THE FORMATION OF
THE CHRISTIAN SCRIPTURES

BOOKS BY MARGARET BAXTER
published by The Westminster Press

Jesus Christ: His Life and His Church

The Formation of the Christian Scriptures

THE FORMATION OF
THE CHRISTIAN SCRIPTURES

Margaret Baxter

The Westminster Press
Philadelphia

First published in Great Britain 1988 by SPCK, Holy Trinity Church, Marylebone Road, London NW1 4DU

The photographs are reproduced by courtesy of Malcolm Bligh (p. 5b); CMS (pp. 5a, 32, 51, 61); the Mansell Collection (pp. 13, 24, 40, 72, 98, 103, 115b); the British Library (pp. 78, 86b); The Britain/Israel Public Affairs Committee (p. 86a); the John Rylands Library (p. 115a); USPG (p. 124); and Camera Press Ltd.

First American edition

Published by The Westminster Press®
Philadelphia, Pennsylvania

PRINTED IN THE UNITED STATES OF AMERICA

9 8 7 6 5 4 3 2 1

Library of Congress Cataloging-in-Publication Data

Baxter, Margaret.
   The formation of the Christian scriptures.

   Bibliography: p.
   Includes index.
   1. Bible. N.T.—Criticism, interpretation, etc.
I. Title.
BS2361.2.B38 1988   226'.07   88-27665
ISBN 0-664-25044-0 (pbk.)

Contents

Preface

I should like to express grateful acknowledgements for the help and advice that I have received from so many people. In particular I want to thank:

The students of the Sierra Leone Church Training Centre and Theological Hall who taught me so much, and without whom this book would not have been conceived, and the colleagues who encouraged my efforts.

The staff of SPCK, without whom it would have remained no more than an idea in the mind. My thanks go especially to Nick Beddow for his enthusiasm and encouragement, and to Daphne Terry for her attention to detail.

Stuart, Ruth, Mary and Paul for their patience over several years.

Those who over the years have shared their own enthusiasm for the study of theology, and encouraged me to do the same. My thanks to David Hinson, whose Introduction to the Old Testament in this series has been a useful teaching aid and provided me with a number of ideas.

The following people who kindly gave their time and their expertise to read the manuscript, and sent their comments and suggestions: The Reverend Dr C. K. Barrett, Professor Emeritus of Durham University; The Rt Reverend Dr R. P. C. Hanson, Professor Emeritus of Manchester University; The Reverend Canon John Hargreaves; The Reverend Canon Rodney Hunter of Zomba Theological College, Malawi; The Reverend Dr Mathew John, Principal of Bishop's College, Calcutta. Their comments were of great value and all have been given careful consideration.

My hope is that this book will be useful for those who are studying the New Testament for the first time, and that it will encourage them to go on to further study at much greater depth.

Nelson, Lancashire 1988   MARGARET BAXTER

About This Book

This is the second volume in a two-volume introduction to the New Testament. The first volume contains an account of events, beginning with Jesus Christ and ending with the leaders of the early Church writing letters to Christians. This second volume begins with the writing of the Gospels, and traces the events which have led to our reading the New Testament in modern translations.

AN INTRODUCTION

In the study of theology the word 'introduction' is often used as a technical expression which refers to questions such as 'Who wrote this book?', 'When did he write it?', 'For whom did he write it?'. Some of these questions are touched on in these two books. However, they are chiefly intended to be an 'introduction' in the general and more usual sense, introducing readers to the background as well as the content of the New Testament, discussing different aspects of its teaching and interpretation, and showing how it reached its present form. Many books about the New Testament, even introductory books, contain technical words without fully explaining them. (This is not only a problem of theology; every subject has its own specialized language.) In this Guide we explain most of the technical terms used as we go along, as well as providing concise definitions of them in Appendix 1.

SPECIAL NOTES

These notes are separate from the text because they relate to more than one section of the book. Readers may want to read the special notes first, or to read them as they work through the book, or to leave them out altogether.

STUDY SUGGESTIONS

Most chapters in the book are divided into two or three sections, with study suggestions at the end of each section. There are four kinds of study suggestion:

Words and Meanings: These are to help readers check their understanding of the words used.

Review of Content: These questions are to help readers check their progress, and discover whether they have remembered and understood what they have read.

Bible Study: These suggestions are to help readers to understand more clearly the form and content of the various New Testament books, and to discover for themselves the relationships between them and between the New Testament itself and the Old Testament. Questions requiring use of a concordance or Bible dictionary are meant for students who possess such books or have access to a library.

Further Study and Discussion: These are to help readers to do further study, and to think out the practical application of what has been learned, in their own lives and in the life of the Church as a whole. These questions are especially useful for group discussions.

The *Key* (p. 134) will enable readers to check their own work on those questions which can be checked in that way.

TECHNICAL TERMS

Appendix 1 (p. 129) provides concise definitions of the technical terms which have been used.

USEFUL ABBREVIATIONS

Appendix 2 (p. 132) 'translates' the various abbreviations used. It also includes abbreviations which are not used in this book, but which readers may find they need as they read other books of theology.

INDEX

The Index includes most of the subjects dealt with in this book, and the names of important people and places.

BIBLE VERSION

This Guide, like the others in the series, is based upon the Revised Standard Version of the Bible.

HELPS TO BIBLE STUDY

Readers will also find the following books helpful.

1. *A Concordance*, which is an alphabetical list of words and names used in the Bible, with references to show the books, chapters and verses where they may be found. A concordance is usually related to a version of the Bible, e.g. *The Oxford Concise Concordance to the RSV*. Students of the Bible find it very helpful to have a concordance of their own.

2. *A Bible Dictionary* contains articles on the topics, places and

people which are found in the Bible, e.g. 'sabbaths'. Most theological libraries have at least one Bible dictionary.
3. *Commentaries.* Most commentaries deal with one book of the Bible (e.g. the Gospel of Mark) which is explained chapter by chapter. There are also some one-volume commentaries which deal with every book in the Bible, and contain general articles about the Bible. A one-volume commentary is a very useful book to possess.

FURTHER READING

INTRODUCTORY BOOKS

D. B. J. Campbell, *The Synoptic Gospels: A Commentary.* New York: Seabury Press, 1969.
Hans von Campenhausen, *The Formation of the Christian Bible.* Tr. by J. A. Baker. Philadelphia: Fortress Press, 1972.
Étienne Charpentier, *How to Read the New Testament.* New York. Crossroad Publishing Co., 1982.
Bruce Chilton, *Beginning New Testament Study.* Grand Rapids: Wm. B. Eerdmans Publishing Co., 1987.
John Drane, *Jesus and the Four Gospels.* New York: Harper & Row, 1979.
Lucas Grollenberg, *Jesus.* Philadelphia: Westminster Press, 1979.
Morna Hooker, *Studying the New Testament.* Minneapolis: Augsburg Publishing House, 1982.
Rosalyn A. Kendrick, *Setting the Foundations.* Amersham, Bucks: Hulton Educational Publications, 1983.
Frederic G. Kenyon, *Our Bible and the Ancient Manuscripts.* Rev. by A. W. Adams. New York: Harper & Brothers, 1958.
O. Jessie Lace, ed., *Understanding the New Testament.* Cambridge Bible Commentary on the New English Bible. New York: Cambridge University Press, 1965.
John Stott, *Understanding the Bible,* 2nd ed. Grand Rapids: Zondervan Publishing House, 1985.

MORE ADVANCED BOOKS

H. C. Key and F. W. Young, *The Living World of the New Testament.* London: Darton, Longman & Todd, 1960.
Alexander Souter, *The Text and Canon of the New Testament.* Ed. by C. S. C. Williams. Naperville, Ill.: Alec R. Allenson, 1954.

Christopher M. Tuckett, *Reading the New Testament: Methods of Interpretation*. London: SPCK, 1987.

USEFUL REFERENCE BOOKS

Concise Oxford Dictionary of the Christian Church, 1977.
The New Bible Dictionary, 2nd ed. (Eerdmans), 1982.
Oxford Bible Atlas, 3rd ed., 1984.
Oxford Concise Concordance to the Revised Standard Version of the Holy Bible, 1962.
A Concise History of the English Bible. New York: American Bible Society, 1986.

1
Why the Gospels Were Written

'These are written that you may believe that Jesus is the Christ, the Son of God, and that believing you may have life in his name.' (John 20.30)

The message which the first followers of Jesus proclaimed was that in Jesus Christ God had fulfilled the promises He made to Israel. He had opened the way of salvation for everybody. This was the good news, the gospel. The word 'gospel' did not originally refer to a book about the life and death of Jesus. It meant the good news that was preached. Even now there is only one gospel. The four books that we call 'Gospels' are really four accounts of the one gospel. Their full names show this: 'The Gospel according to St Matthew'. 'The Gospel according to St Mark', etc.

THE NEED FOR THE WRITTEN GOSPEL

In Volume 1 of this Introduction to the New Testament we saw how the Church began, and how it had two main jobs to do. The people who had known and followed Jesus when He was alive had to proclaim to others the good news of what God had done. When those who heard the message believed and were baptized, they had to be taught what it meant to be a follower of Jesus. We saw how the New Testament letters were a part of the Church's teaching ministry. They were all addressed to Christian groups or individuals, and were written to meet immediate needs, and answer immediate questions.

The Gospels contain material for both the preaching ministry and the teaching ministry of the Church. They were written as handbooks. One of their main purposes was to provide material for Christians who were preaching the gospel to outsiders.

STRUCTURED ACCOUNTS IN BOOK FORM

The Gospels are real *books*. They were not written in the heat of the moment, as at least some of the letters were. There is a sense in which we may say that the Gospels 'grew'. They were developed over a number of years to meet the preaching and teaching needs of the Church. Probably there were several editions of all of them, before the final editions which have come down to us. We could compare them with this book, which began as teaching notes. The teaching notes were revised, and some of them revised again. Then, because of a need, a

1

book was planned. A first draft was written, then a second draft. The one book was divided into two books, and finally they have been published. Once that has happened there is no more need for the teaching notes, or for the earlier drafts of a book, and they can be thrown away. Writing a book is entirely different from writing a letter.

A CHANGING SITUATION

The first Christians had no need of written accounts of Jesus' life. They had known Him. They had seen Him die, and then had experienced His risen presence. The people who heard the first disciples preach and were baptized also had no need of such accounts. They heard about Jesus from those who had known Him. The apostles were with them all the time, and they provided a living contact with Jesus. All of those very early Christians were waiting impatiently for Jesus to return and judge the world. So they were busy proclaiming the gospel to others before His expected coming. They had no time to spend writing down what He had said and done.

As the years went by, however, the situation gradually changed.

1. THE RAPID SPREAD OF THE CHURCH

As the good news about Jesus spread beyond Palestine into the towns and villages of the Roman Empire, it was no longer possible for every new Christian to be taught by one of the Twelve. Many Christians never even saw an apostle. If their teacher had himself been taught by an apostle, that was something to be proud of. A new generation of Christian preachers and teachers began to grow up who had never met an apostle. They needed to be provided with good reliable information about Jesus' life, death and teaching.

2. THE SECOND COMING DID NOT HAPPEN

As we saw in Volume 1, the *parousia* did not happen as soon as Jesus' followers had expected (Vol. 1, pp. 123, 125). When Christians realized that Jesus' teaching about His return could be interpreted in other ways, they began to make longer-term plans for life on this earth.

3. THE DEATH OF THE APOSTLES

Some of the Apostles had died fairly soon after the death of Jesus Himself. James the son of Zebedee had been put to death by Herod Agrippa (Acts 12.2; see also Vol. 1, ch. 2), and only a miracle had prevented Peter from being executed at the same time (Acts 12.3–11). We have very little information about the death of the apostles. According to the tradition of the Church Peter and Paul both died as martyrs in Rome, probably when Nero was emperor (see Vol. 1, ch. 8). Some probably died natural deaths, from illness or old age, others died

2

as martyrs. Certainly the apostles were not going to be with the Church for ever to keep a check on the stories that were told about Jesus.

This changing situation meant that as time went by Christians began to have more need of information that was written down.

THE NEEDS OF PREACHERS AND TEACHERS

When the apostles themselves proclaimed the good news about Jesus they had all the information they needed, since they had been eye-witnesses of the events which they proclaimed. However, even among the first converts there were people who had never seen Jesus. They could only tell the stories which they had heard. Possibly Christians collected and wrote down information about Jesus at a very early date. No one knows exactly what they wrote, or how early they wrote it. However some of the following may have been written down within twenty years of Jesus' crucifixion.

1. *Collections of Old Testament quotations* which the Christians thought pointed to Jesus. Some biblical scholars call such texts 'proof texts', because they were believed to 'prove' who Jesus was, e.g. 'Thou wilt not abandon my soul to Hades, Nor let thy Holy One see corruption' (Ps. 16.10 as quoted in Acts 2.27). Peter quoted this verse from the Psalms to 'prove' the resurrection of Jesus. The first two chapters of Matthew's Gospel contain a great many proof texts.

2. *An account of Jesus' suffering and death.* The proclamation of Jesus' death and resurrection was the central feature of the *kerygma* (see Vol. 1, pp. 60, 61). Preachers were telling what God had done, and they needed to know about the main events.

3. *Stories about the miracles of Jesus.* The miracles fulfilled the promises of the Old Testament, and pointed to Jesus as the Messiah.

4. *Collections of the sayings of Jesus,* to be used in teaching new Christians.

GOSPELS COMPILED AND EDITED

'Inasmuch as many have undertaken to compile a narrative of the things which have been accomplished among us, just as they were delivered to us by those who from the beginning were eyewitnesses and ministers of the word, it seemed good to me also, having followed all things closely for some time past, to write an orderly account for you' (Luke 1.1–3). This introduction to St Luke's Gospel is worth careful study. To 'compile' is to gather information or stories together into a useful form. According to Luke, 'many' had compiled a narrative 'of the things which have been accomplished among us'. They collected their information from 'those who from the beginning were eyewitnesses'. Luke said that it seemed good to him also 'to write an orderly account'. We might deduce from this that he did not consider those early compilations to be 'orderly'. Luke himself was not an eyewitness, so he had to depend on other people for his information. He probably used some of the accounts which other people had compiled.

We have no way of knowing how many accounts Luke knew. One of them may have been made by Mark. Luke and Mark were both with Paul when he was in prison (Philemon 23). Nor have we any way of knowing how many drafts of his Gospel Luke may have made before the final one that we have in the New Testament. Luke and the other Church leaders who collected and wrote down stories about Jesus did not think they were writing 'Scripture'. They were simply providing tools for the men and women who would preach and teach in the future. If Luke obtained some new information, or thought of a different way of presenting his material, he could revise what he had written. In some of the Gospels there are clues to what an earlier edition may have been like, but generally speaking we cannot tell how many stages the Gospels passed through. All we have are the finished products, and they may have reached their present shape over many years. Other people may have edited the Gospels besides the original authors. As in the case of the New Testament letters, possible editorial additions to the Gospels are called 'redactions' (see Vol. 1, p. 88).

THE GOSPELS AS KERYGMA

The greater part of each of the four Gospels is devoted to an account of the last week of Jesus' life, and especially the events of the final twenty-four hours. We call such an account of Jesus' suffering and death a 'passion narrative'. This was the heart of the message which the Christians proclaimed to non-believers. St Paul reminded the Corinthian Christians of the message he had proclaimed: 'I would remind you brethren, in what terms I preached to you the gospel ... For I delivered to you as of first importance what I also received, that Christ died for our sins in accordance with the Scripture' (1 Cor. 15.1–3).

There are sixteen chapters in St Mark's Gospel. Ten of them are devoted to an account of Jesus' life and teaching. Six are devoted to the passion narrative. The other three Gospels are all longer than Mark. Their writers have included more stories about Jesus' ministry, and more of His teaching, yet they have also told the story of Jesus' passion in great detail.

The authors' stated intentions also show us that the Gospels were written to proclaim the good news. Luke stated that he had written his orderly account 'that you may know the truth' (Luke 1.4). Mark began his Gospel with the words, 'The beginning of the gospel of Jesus Christ' (Mark 1.1). The writer of the Fourth Gospel stated his aim even more

4

'The Church leaders who recorded the events of Jesus' life, and wrote down His sayings, were providing tools for those who would preach and teach in many different situations in the future' – a Church leader of today expounding a Bible lesson in a local Church in Britain, or Mothers' Union members in Southern Sudan, who have travelled many miles through areas torn by guerilla fighting to preach and pray with fellow-members in isolated villages.

clearly: 'that you may believe that Jesus is the Christ, the Son of God, and that believing you may have life in his name' (John 20.31).

THE GOSPELS AS THEOLOGICAL BOOKS

The Gospels are about God, and what God has done. They are 'orderly accounts', but they are orderly *theological* accounts, written for theological purposes. We may understand this more clearly if we notice what the writers *did not* intend their books to be.

(a) The Gospels are not detailed biographical accounts of Jesus's life. If we go to the biography section of a library, and choose a book about Mahatma Gandhi, for example, we expect to read about his home and his childhood, what he looked like, the friends he made as he was growing up, and the various influences that affected his life and character. When we read the Gospels we find very little information of this sort. The Gospel writers were not interested in such information. Only Matthew and Luke tell about any of the events surrounding Jesus' birth. Luke alone records a single incident from Jesus' childhood. The Gospel writers tell us nothing about the greater part of His life. We discover almost by chance that Jesus had 'brothers and sisters', and that He had worked as a carpenter.

(b) Gospels are not books written by professional historians. The Gospels are full of historical events, but Luke was the only Gospel writer who was really interested in the details of history. He gave a rough date for Jesus' birth, and a more precise date for His baptism (Luke 2.1–2; 3.1–2). Yet even Luke was more interested in theology than in history.

When God's Son was born as a human being, He entered human history, and so the Gospels and the creeds contain many historical facts. When we say 'crucified under Pontius Pilate', it is a way of saying that the crucifixion was a real event in history. Since Jesus lived in Palestine in the first century AD, we can find the names of people like Herod and Tiberius Caesar in the Gospels (see Vol. 1, ch. 2). As the Gospel writers worked to carry out their main purpose, they were bound to include historical facts. But their main purpose was always to show that God was in Jesus Christ, so that people would believe in Him and become His followers. It was not the Gospel writers' main concern to tell historical details, or to tell the events of Jesus' life in the order in which they happened.

THE EVANGELISTS

'*Evangelion*' is a Greek word meaning 'good news'. An 'evangelist' is someone who brings good news. Timothy was told. 'Do the work of an evangelist' (2 Tim. 4.5). The writers of the Gospels brought good news through their writings, so they are also called evangelists. Just as modern evangelists are different from each other, all having their own individual approach, so the writers of the four Gospels were all different. They told the same good news, and wrote about the same Jesus, but each one of them wrote from his own point of view, and had in his mind the particular needs of the people for whom he was writing.

STUDY SUGGESTIONS

WORDS AND MEANINGS

1. Which of the following sorts of book are usually 'compiled'?
   (a) A hymn book   (b) A poem   (c) A dictionary   (d) A concordance   (e) A collection of short stories   (f) A novel
2. What does it mean when a book is described as having been 'revised'?
3. What is meant by 'long-term plans'? In what way are they different from 'short-term' plans?
4. In the study of the Gospels, what is meant by the phrase 'passion narrative'?
5. Explain why the writers of the four Gospels are also called 'evangelists'.

REVIEW OF CONTENT

6. What do biblical scholars mean by the term 'a proof text'?
7. (a) Give two reasons why the early Christians did not feel the need for a written gospel.
   (b) Give three reasons why the Church began to need written accounts of the gospel.
8. Which of the following details about Jesus can be found in the Gospels, and which cannot?
   (a) His mother's name.
   (b) His date of birth.
   (c) His appearance.
   (d) Stories about His birth.
   (e) An account of His circumcision.
   (f) The name of the rabbi who taught Him at school.
   (g) An account of His life as a young man.
9. Why is such a large part of each Gospel devoted to the last week of Jesus' life?
10. Which of the four Gospels gives a date for the beginning of Jesus' ministry?

BIBLE STUDY

11. Read the account of an apostle being chosen to take Judas

Iscariot's place in the Twelve, in Acts 1.15–26. How much of Jesus' ministry was an apostle required to have witnessed?

12. Find as many Old Testament quotations as you can in Matthew, chapter 2, and give their OT references.

13. Read Luke's introduction to his Gospel (Luke 1.1–4).
    (a) What were 'the things which have been accomplished among us'?
    (b) Why did Luke think he was a suitable person to write an account?

14. What did Paul mean when he used the expression 'the gospel' in his letters? What is the connection between the gospel that Paul wrote about, and the four Gospels in the New Testament?

15. All four Gospels contain the story of Jesus turning over the money-changers' tables in the Temple. Which of the evangelists put it at the end of Jesus' ministry, and which put it at the beginning?

FURTHER STUDY AND DISCUSSION

16. How far is it important for us to know the correct order of events in the ministry of Jesus? Give reasons for your answer.

17. None of us who are alive today are eye-witnesses to the ministry, death and resurrection of Jesus. How do we know whether any or all of it is true?

18. A student training for ordination once said during a discussion with his tutor: 'It is not that we are against change. It is just that we shouldn't do anything we haven't done before.' What do you think that ordinand was really trying to say about change and tradition?

FACTS AND THEORIES

As we study the four Gospel accounts of Jesus, we shall begin to notice various facts about the similarities and differences between them, e.g. the fact that there are no stories about the birth of Jesus in Mark's Gospel. Anyone who has a Bible can check to see if this is true. When we are in possession of the facts we may think of a theory to explain them. One theory is that Luke used other people's accounts of Jesus when he wrote his Gospel.

Biblical scholars have worked out many theories by which they try to explain the facts which they have discovered in the Gospels. Theories are never certainties, and they are being changed all the time. Scholars often alter their own or other people's theories in order to explain facts which had been forgotten or not noticed before. Sometimes a theory may be quickly rejected by most scholars because they do not consider that it is a satisfactory explanation of the facts.

AN ACCURATE KNOWLEDGE OF THE TEXT

People who grow up within the Church hear the Gospel stories over and over again. We may think that we know the Gospels well, but it is easy for us to remember what we think is there, instead of what is really there. We are especially influenced by the following things.

COMPOSITE STORIES

Often the story we have in our minds is made up of several different accounts. We can see this by looking at the story of the rich young ruler. It appears in three of the Gospels, and we can set it out in columns to show the differences and similarities between the three accounts (see p. 10).

These three accounts are very similar to each other, but we can notice small differences. Only Matthew describes the man as young. Without Matthew's account we might easily imagine a middle-aged or elderly man: 'All these I have observed from my youth' (Mark 10.20; Luke 18.21). Only Luke tells us that the man was a ruler. The name that we give to the story—the rich young ruler—shows that we have a mixture of all three accounts in our minds.

Another example of the way in which details are gathered from different Gospels are the 'seven words' which Jesus spoke from the cross. The greatest number of these 'words' that can be found in any one of the Gospels is four. The *seven* words have been gathered from all four Gospels.

MORE POPULAR VERSIONS

People are often more familiar with one evangelist's account of a story than with the others. For example, in the story of Jesus being tempted in the wilderness, many of us would list the three things which the devil tempted Jesus to do, in this order: to turn stones into bread; to throw Himself from a pinnacle of the Temple; and to worship the devil. This is because most people are familiar with the story as it appears in Matthew's Gospel, which has always been a very popular Gospel, especially for reading in Church services. But in Luke's account the order is different. According to Luke the devil tempted Jesus to worship him before he suggested that He throw Himself off a pinnacle of the Temple.

The most popular version of the feeding of the Five Thousand is the account in John's Gospel, although our idea of that occasion is also influenced by the accounts in the other Gospels.

TRADITION

Many traditions about Jesus and the other people about whom we read

THE RICH YOUNG RULER

Mark 10.17–22	Matt. 19.16–22	Luke 18.18–23
A man ran up and knelt before him, and asked him, 'Good Teacher, what must I do to inherit eternal life?' And Jesus said to him, 'Why do you call me good? No one is good but God alone. You know the commandments:	One came up to him, saying, 'Teacher, what good deed must I do to have eternal life?' And he said to him 'Why do you ask me about what is good? One there is who is good. If you would enter life, keep the commandments.' He said to him, 'Which?' and Jesus said, 'You	A ruler asked him, 'Good Teacher, what shall I do to inherit eternal life?' And Jesus said to him, 'Why do you call me good?' No one is good but God alone. You know the commandments:
"Do not kill, Do not commit adultery, Do not steal, Do not bear false witness, Do not defraud, Honour your father and mother." '	shall not kill, You shall not commit adultery, You shall not steal, You shall not bear false witness. Honour your father and mother, You shall love your neighbour as yourself'	'Do not commit adultery, Do not kill, Do not steal, Do not bear false witness, Honour your father and mother." '
And he said to him. 'Teacher, all these I have observed from my youth.' And Jesus looking upon him loved him, and said to him, 'You lack one thing; go, sell what you have, and give to the poor, and you will have treasure in heaven; and come, follow me.' At that saying his countenance fell, and he went away sorrowful; for he had great possessions.	The young man said to him 'All these I have observed; what do I still lack?' Jesus said to him, 'If you would be perfect, go, sell what you possess and give to the poor, and you will have treasure in heaven; and come, follow me.' When the young man heard this he went away sorrowful; for he had great possessions.	And he said, 'All these I have observed from my youth.' And when Jesus heard it, he said to him, 'One thing you still lack. Sell all that you have and distribute to the poor, and you will have treasure in heaven; and come, follow me.' But he heard this and became sad, for he was very rich.

in the New Testament have been handed on in the Church, but do not appear in the books which are included in the Bible. Many of them are about Mary and the events surrounding the birth of Jesus. Others are about His childhood, e.g. there is a tradition that Joseph died when Jesus was still a boy, though there is no record of it in the Gospel stories.

SOME FACTS ABOUT THE GOSPELS

We can sort out the material in the Gospels according to whether we can find it in one, two, three or four Gospels.

MATERIAL FOUND IN ALL FOUR GOSPELS

Some of the Gospel material appears in all four Gospels. They all contain information about John the Baptist. They all contain an account of Jesus feeding 5,000 people. The broad outline of the story of the crucifixion is the same in all four Gospels, as well as some of the details. For example, all four evangelists tell that Jesus was crucified between two other people.

MATERIAL FOUND IN THREE GOSPELS

Many of the stories about Jesus appear in Matthew, Mark, and also in Luke. For example, these three evangelists all tell the stories of Jesus healing a leper, of Jairus's daughter, of a woman with a flow of blood (Matt. 8.2–4; 9.18–26). The three accounts of the rich young ruler are set out on p. 10 so that the similarities and differences between them are easily seen. The similarities are very clear. In many cases all three evangelists have used the same words. If we were to buy three newspapers and read their accounts of one event, we should not expect to find so many identical details.

As well as containing a lot of similar material, Matthew, Mark and Luke describe events in the same general order. They describe how Jesus began His ministry in Galilee, and did not go to Jerusalem until the final visit which ended in His death. For this reason Matthew, Mark and Luke are often called the 'Synoptic Gospels', meaning that they give a similar view of Jesus.

Some Bible publishers issue these three Synoptic Gospels in what is called a 'Synopsis', that is to say a book in which they are set out together in a series of tables like that on p. 10, to show the similarities and differences between them. The first table in a Synopsis sets out the whole of St Mark's Gospel, and shows the matching passages in Matthew and Luke in parallel columns alongside. The second table sets out the passages of Matthew's Gospel which did not appear in the first table, showing the matching passages in Luke. The third table does the same thing for Luke's Gospel.

There are some stories and sayings which appear in one or more of the Synoptic Gospels and also in John's Gospel. For example, Matthew, Mark and John all contain an account of Jesus walking on the water (Matt. 14.22–39; Mark 6.47–52; John 6.16–21). In such cases we do not find the same strong likenesses between the words that we sometimes find in stories which appear in all three Synoptic Gospels. Biblical scholars disagree about whether or not the writer of John's Gospel was familiar with any of the Synoptic Gospels.

MATERIAL FOUND IN TWO GOSPELS

Some of the stories which appear in Mark appear also in Matthew or in Luke, but not in both of them. Matthew and Mark have the story of the Syrophoenician woman (Matt. 15.21–28; Mark 7.24–30). Mark and Luke tell the story of the Widow's Mite (Mark 12.41–44; Luke 21.1–4).

A number of Jesus' parables and sayings, and a few stories, are to be found only in Matthew and Luke, e.g. the story of Jesus' temptation in the wilderness. There may be differences, such as the order of the temptations, but often the words are remarkably similar. Here, for example, are the words of the centurion as recorded by Matthew and Luke in the story of the centurion's servant:

Matthew 8.8–10	*Luke 7.6–8*
'Lord, I am not worthy to have you come under my roof; but only say the word, and my servant will be healed For I am a man set under authority, with soldiers under me; and I say to one, "Go," and he goes, and to another, "Come," and he comes, and to my slave, "Do this," and he does it.'	'Lord, do not trouble yourself, for I am not worthy to have you come under my roof; therefore I did not presume to come to you. But say the word, and let my servant be healed. For I am a man set under authority, with soldiers under me: and I say to one, "Go," and he goes; and to another, "Come," and he comes; and to my slave, "Do this," and he does it.'

MATERIAL FOUND IN ONLY ONE GOSPEL

Each of the Gospels contains material which does not appear in any other Gospel. Mark, which is the shortest Gospel, contains the fewest stories which do not appear anywhere else. Most of what appears in Mark also appears in either Matthew or in Luke, if not in both. One of

'We can sort out the material in the Gospels according to the similarities and differences between them.' Sixth-century mosaic portraits in the Church of San Vitale in Ravenna, showing the four evangelists at work, include this one of St Matthew holding a codex, seated at his writing table with pens and ink and a leather box full of scrolls.

the few stories which appears only in Mark is the account of Jesus healing a deaf man (Mark 7.32–36).

John's Gospel contain's the most material which cannot be found in any other Gospel. One example is the story of the wedding at Cana (John 2.1–11), but in fact the greater part of the material in John is found only in that Gospel.

Matthew and Luke too, each contain a good deal of material not found in the other Gospels. Although they both contain accounts of the birth of Jesus, the two accounts are very different from each other, and each of these Gospels has stories, parables and other teaching which is peculiar to itself. For example, only Luke has the story of Jesus staying with Martha and Mary, and the parable of the Good Samaritan (Luke 10.38–42, 29–37). Only Matthew tells the story of the coin in the fish's mouth, and the parable of the labourers in the vineyard (Matt. 17.24–27; 20.1–16).

IDEAS AND THEORIES

FORM CRITICISM

Earlier this century some German theologians, especially M. Dibelius (d. 1947) and R. Bultmann (d. 1976), developed a method of studying the Gospels which we call in English 'form criticism'. They analysed the Gospel stories according to their 'form' or shape. The story of Jesus eating with tax-collectors and sinners, for example, contains very few details. It simply provides a background for the saying of Jesus with which it ends: 'Those who are well have no need of a physician, but those who are sick; I came not to call the righteous, but sinners' (Mark 2.15–17). Form critics call this story a 'pronouncement story'. In contrast, many stories of Jesus' miracles are full of details, e.g. in the account of His stilling the storm, 'He was in the stern, asleep on the cushion.' Mark 4.35–41. Form critics class such stories as 'miracle stories'. Stories about healings in particular seem to follow the same pattern: the exact situation of the sick person is described (perhaps as a way of convincing readers that the story is true). Jesus' action of healing and the words which He spoke are recorded, and the effectiveness of the healing is reported.

The form critics argued that in the early Church each story about Jesus, each parable or saying, was a separate unit, told many times by preachers and teachers, and in this way gaining its 'form'. Although the writers of the Synoptic Gospels do not always record the stories of Jesus in the same order, they all place the story of the woman with the flow of blood in the middle of the story of the healing of Jairus's daughter (e.g. Matt. 9.18–30). The two stories were joined together to make a single unit, probably long before the story was written down.

In tracing the Gospel stories back to the oral tradition (see Special Note A, p. 19), the form critics emphasized the importance of the spoken word in the making of the Gospels. Bultmann sometimes gave the impression that he did not consider the Gospels to be historically reliable. However, form criticism has made biblical scholars aware of the different forms used, especially in the Synoptic Gospels. It has emphasized the 'life-situations' in which the stories were originally told (see Vol. 1, ch. 5). It has made it clear that the Gospels were concerned with faith in Jesus rather than in factual knowledge about Him.

Form criticism has become a tool to help people to understand what sort of books the Gospels are.

THE DOCUMENTARY THEORY

At the same time as the form critical method was being developed in Germany the English theologian B. H. Streeter published some important works setting out his theories about the Gospels. In particular he had noticed:

1. The amazing similarity in the words of stories and sayings which occur in two or more of the Synoptic Gospels.

2. That most of Mark's material appears in either Matthew or Luke or both.

Streeter believed this meant that when Matthew and Luke compiled their Gospels they both had a copy of Mark's Gospel, and that both used the information which Mark had already collected and written down. He thought that both must also have used another document which contained stories such as the centurion's servant. For convenience he called this document 'Q'. 'Q' would have been a collection of sayings and stories about Jesus which Churches used for teaching. Streeter also thought that Matthew and Luke must each have had yet another, separate, document to draw upon. He called Matthew's special document 'M', and Luke's, 'L'.

This 'documentary' theory has had a great influence on the study of the Gospels. Biblical scholars accept that there is a close connection between the Synoptic Gospels, and consider that Mark is probably the earliest of them. Most scholars also agree that there must have been a book like 'Q' which Matthew and Luke used, although its existence cannot be proved. But few people still think that 'M' or 'L' were single documents, and some do not think they were documents at all. However, the letters 'M' and 'L' have become a useful way to distinguish Matthew's and Luke's special material.

A MULTI-DOCUMENTARY THEORY

Even biblical scholars can only make guesses (i.e. theories) about how the Gospels reached their present form. Each theory explains some of the available facts, and leaves other facts unexplained. For example, the theory that Matthew and Luke both used Mark answers some questions, but it raises others. If Matthew was copying material from Mark, this explains the similarity in the words; but it does not explain why he added the detail that the rich man who came to Jesus was *young*. If he already knew the story, why did he use Mark's account? In the story of Jesus' transfiguration, why does Luke state that Jesus went up the mountain 'eight days after' (Luke 9.28) when Mark has 'after six days' (Mark 9.2)?

The theory that Matthew and Luke used Mark's Gospel as we know it led to the belief that they wrote their Gospels at a later date, after Mark's Gospel had been copied out many times and become well known. However, we should not forget that the leaders of the early Church knew each other. We have already noticed that Mark and Luke were both with Paul when he wrote to Philemon. Possibly Matthew and Luke both used earlier versions of Mark's Gospel. Perhaps all three of them used the same written collection of stories.

Although the early Christians felt no need for Gospels as such, they may have collected and written down information about Jesus from a very early date. We have noticed Luke's statement that 'many' had compiled narratives about Jesus. Instead of using only three or four documents, as Streeter suggested, Luke may have used an early version of Mark, plus 'Q', and also several documents which Mark and Matthew did not know, as well as material which he had heard from others, and wrote down himself.

The different stages of the Gospel stories and of the Gospels themselves remain a matter for theories. What we have in the New Testament are the final editions. In the following chapters we shall look more carefully at each of the Gospels to see what sort of books they are and what needs their writers were trying to meet.

STUDY SUGGESTIONS

WORDS AND MEANINGS

1. What is the 'broad outline' of a story?
2. Many books about the Gospels refer to material which is 'peculiar' to one Gospel. What does the word 'peculiar' mean when used in this way?
3. What does the phrase 'historically reliable' mean?
4. What is meant by 'separate unit' in the sentence, 'In the early Church each story about Jesus was a separate unit'?

REVIEW

5. Explain the difference between a 'fact' and a 'theory'.
6. Explain why Matthew, Mark and Luke are called 'the Synoptic Gospels'.
7. (a) Which Gospel contains the *least* 'peculiar' material? (see question 2)
   (b) Which Gospel contains the *most* peculiar material?
8. Why are some Gospel stories called 'pronouncement stories'?
9. Describe three ways in which 'form criticism' has made a valuable contribution to the study of the Gospels.
10. (a) What did Streeter use 'M' to mean in his writing?
    (b) What do most biblical scholars use 'M' to mean today?

BIBLE STUDY

(*Note*: A concordance, if you have one, will be helpful for questions 11, 12, and 13.)
11. Here is a list of 'facts' which many people believe are found in the Gospels. See whether you can find them, and give chapter and verse references for the ones you do find.
    (a) Three wise men came to see the infant Jesus.
    (b) Jesus was born in a stable.
    (c) The baby Jesus was laid in a manger.
    (d) Jesus taught that it was wrong to drink alcohol.
12. Which of the following stories about the birth of Jesus are to be found in Matthew's Gospel and which are to be found in Luke?
    (a) An angel announces to Mary that she will have a son.
    (b) An angel tells Joseph in a dream that he should not divorce Mary.
    (c) Wise men came to worship Jesus.
    (d) Shepherds came to worship Jesus.
    (e) Joseph took Mary and the baby to Egypt.
13. The Gospels contain four accounts of Jesus feeding a great crowd of 5000 people. One of them appears in Matt. 14.13–21. Use the cross-reference system in your Bible to find the other three accounts, and find out:
    (a) Which account states that women and children were present as well as men?
    (b) In which account did Andrew introduce Jesus to a boy who gave Him five barley loaves and two fishes?
    (c) Which writer said that the people sat down 'by hundreds and by fifties'?
    (d) Which accounts state that it was a grassy place?
14. Find the story of Jairus's daughter (Matt. 9.18–26) in all three

Synoptic Gospels, and write it out in three parallel columns so as to show the similarity between the three accounts.

15. Compare the Lord's Prayer in Matt. 6.9–13 and Luke 11.2–4.
    (a) Which phrases appear in both versions?
    (b) Which phrases appear only in Matthew?
    (c) Which phrases appear only in Luke?

FURTHER STUDY AND DISCUSSION

16. What difference does it make if we accept that Matthew and Luke used a version of Mark when they wrote their Gospels? Does it make their accounts more or less reliable? Or does it make no difference? Give your reasons.

17. Tell a story to a friend, and then ask that friend to re-tell the story. Listen carefully and note any differences in the re-telling. Discuss how these differences have come about. Now look at the story of the feeding of the 5,000 in all four Gospels. Note the differences. How do you think those differences have come about?

18. Some people argue that we cannot believe the Gospels because there are so many differences between the four accounts. How would you answer this criticism?

Special Note A
Oral Tradition

When stories about past events, beliefs, and customs are passed on by word of mouth, rather than by writing them down, we say that they exist in an 'oral tradition'.

Historical scholars who study past events in the life of peoples whose history has not been written down have learned to value 'oral tradition', although such traditions may be about events that happened centuries earlier. From the studies of such scholars we may learn what things to look for in oral tradition.

1. We should consider the origin of a tradition. There are three possible ways in which a tradition can begin:

(a) The first teller actually saw the event, i.e. he was an eyewitness.

(b) The first teller of the tradition invented the story.

(c) It was a rumour. e.g. a chief is ill, and the rumour goes around that he is dead.

2. We should consider the 'chain of transmission', that is, the ways in which it has been handed down:

(a) How many people were involved in passing the story on? The shorter the chain of transmission is, the more reliable the story will be.

(b) Does the story come from a reliable source?

3. We should consider the purpose of the tradition.

(a) Important events and people are more accurately remembered than unimportant events.

(b) All religious traditions are passed on with great care, often to people who have been especially trained to remember them.

(c) Official traditions are usually controlled by people in authority. It may be to their advantage to twist the facts.

4. We should consider the form of the tradition. There are 'fixed forms' and 'free forms'.

A *fixed* form is where the actual words used are important, e.g. in (a) Poems, (b) Proverbs, (c) religious or magic rites.

A *free* form is where the actual words may be changed in the telling, e.g. in stories or narrative, where the main details of the story are fixed, but the words may be changed every time it is told.

5. We should consider whether the tradition contains any aids to memory, e.g.:

(a) Poetry is always easier to remember than prose.

(b) Anything that is repeated frequently will be more easily remembered.

(c) Key words and catch phrases can help the memory.

STUDY SUGGESTIONS

WORD STUDY

1. Explain briefly the meaning of the following phrases:
   (a) oral tradition
   (b) chain of transmission
2. What is the meaning of the following words as they are used in this special note?
   (a) origin (b) reliable (c) source (d) rumour (e) advantage
   (f) rites

REVIEW OF CONTENT

3. In what sort of societies are people dependent on oral tradition?
4. Which sorts of events are most likely to be passed on accurately by word of mouth?
5. What is the meaning of 'fixed form' traditions? Give two examples of fixed form traditions.
6. Are 'official traditions' likely to be more accurate or less accurate than others, and why?

BIBLE STUDY

7. Read the story of the Transfiguration in Mark 9.2–8, and say, if you can:
   (a) Was Mark himself an eyewitness of that event?
   (b) From what source could Mark have heard the story?
   (c) For what purpose was the story told?
   (d) What if anything, would Mark or anyone else have gained by twisting the facts?
8. Consider the tradition, recorded in Matthew's Gospel, that Pilate authorized soldiers to guard Jesus' tomb (Matt. 27.65).
   (a) Is there any reason to think that the other Gospel writers knew this tradition?
   (b) Say how you yourself think the story might have originated, and give your reasons.
9. Read the words of Jesus at the Last Supper as recorded by Paul in 1 Cor. 11.23–25, which most Churches repeat at the Service of Holy Communion. Say whether you consider the following statements about them to be true or false, and give your reasons.
   (a) Paul heard Jesus say the words.
   (b) One or more of the apostles told Paul that Jesus had spoken those words.
   (c) The actual words of Jesus were considered important.
   (d) The words were part of a religious tradition, and were therefore passed on with care.

FURTHER STUDY AND DISCUSSION

10. 'The Gospels are second-hand accounts of the memories of uneducated Galilean peasants, and therefore totally unreliable.' How would you respond to such a criticism?
11. (a) Persuade one or two friends or fellow-students to join you in each writing an account of an event at which you and they were present together. Then compare the accounts to see how far: (i) they agree about the basic facts, (ii) they include the same details. (b) Choose a hymn or chorus which you know well, and write it out from memory. Then compare it with your hymnbook. What does this exercise show about how your memory works?
12. Imagine you are telling someone about an amazing event you have witnessed. What could you do to convince that person that your story is true?

2
The Gospel According to Mark

Most New Testament scholars today accept that Mark's Gospel was the earliest of the four to be written. It is also the shortest, having only sixteen chapters. For both these reasons students usually begin their study of the Gospels by looking at Mark.

AUTHORSHIP: LINKS WITH PETER AND PAUL

Unlike most of the New Testament letters, the Gospels do not contain in the text the names of the people who wrote them. The 'titles' of the Gospels as they appear in the Bible were added later, and they give only the names of the people who were generally believed to have written them. From earliest times the second Gospel was believed to have been written by John Mark.

MARK IN THE NEW TESTAMENT

John Mark, whom Paul described as a cousin of Barnabas (Col. 4.10), is mentioned eight times in the New Testament. His mother lived in Jerusalem, and Christians met to pray in her house (Acts 12.12). When Paul and Barnabas set out on their first missionary journey they took Mark with them, but for reasons which we do not know he left them after they had visited Cyprus, and returned to Jerusalem (Acts 13.13). Paul was unhappy about Mark's leaving them, and refused to take him on his second journey (Acts 15.37–40).

Mark and Paul must have been reconciled later, for in his letters Paul describes Mark as a fellow worker, a comfort to him, and a useful companion: 'Epaphras sends greetings to you, and so do Mark, Aristarchus, Demas and Luke, my fellow workers. (Philemon 23–24). 'Get Mark and bring him along with you; for he is very useful in serving me' (2 Tim. 4.11).

One New Testament reference associates Mark with Peter and the Church in Rome: 'She who is at Babylon, who is likewise chosen, sends you greetings; and so does my son Mark' (1 Peter 5.13).

MARK IN THE TRADITION OF THE CHURCH

We do not know whether Mark was a disciple during Jesus' lifetime. However, according to tradition he was a close friend of Peter, who was not only one of the Twelve, but also one of the three disciples who were closest to Jesus. Christians have long believed that Mark wrote down Peter's memories of Jesus. There is also an ancient tradition that after

Peter had been killed as a martyr in Rome, Mark went to Egypt, and became the first bishop of Alexandria. Mark is held in high honour by the Coptic Christians of Egypt.

TWO EARLY STATEMENTS ABOUT MARK'S GOSPEL

Papias was a leader of the Church in Hierapolis in Asia Minor, who died in about AD 130. Some of his writings have survived to this day. Papias wrote: 'The Elder said, "Mark, having become the interpreter of Peter, wrote down accurately everything that he remembered, without however recording in order, everything that was done or said by Christ."'

Clement of Alexandria was born about twenty years after Papias died. He was a student of philosophy and Christianity, who went to Alexandria to study theology and eventually became head of the school of theology there. In about AD 200 Clement wrote: 'As for Mark then, during Peter's stay in Rome he wrote an account of the Lord's doings, not, however, declaring all of them ... but selecting what he thought most useful for increasing the faith of those who were being instructed. But when Peter died a martyr, Mark came over to Alexandria, bringing both his own notes and those of Peter, from which he transferred to his former book the things suitable for whatever makes for progress towards knowledge. Thus he composed a more spiritual Gospel for the use of those who were being perfected.'

Other Christian writers, who lived later than Papias and Clement, associated Mark with Peter, with Rome and with the second Gospel. Scholars do not always agree about the value of ancient traditions, which often raise questions which cannot now be answered, e.g. Did Papias write down a widely held belief about Mark, or was he giving his own opinion? What did Clement mean when he wrote about 'a more spiritual Gospel'? Were later writers influenced by what Papias had written?

EVIDENCE IN THE GOSPEL

The writers of the Gospels do not tell us about themselves; their purpose was to proclaim Jesus. We have seen that they were not primarily interested in the biographical details of Jesus' life. They had even less reason to tell about their own lives, especially if they were people who had not followed Jesus in His lifetime. Just as the way in which the Gospels reached their present form remains a mystery, so do the writers of the Gospels.

All we can say about Mark is that what we find in his Gospel could fit with the tradition that he was a friend of Peter. Many of the stories in Mark's Gospel are full of details which Peter might have remembered and passed on to Mark. For example, Mark records that when 5,000

'According to tradition Mark was a close friend and interpreter of Peter, and Paul described him as his fellow worker. Mark believed Jesus to be the Messiah, but in his Gospel the disciples only call Him "Teacher".' A mosaic of about AD 400 in a Church in Rome reflects all this, with Christ as Teacher seated between Peter and Paul in the heavenly Jerusalem, and the 'living creatures' of Revelation 4 above.

people sat down to be fed by Jesus, the grass was green (Mark 6.39). This is something that Peter might have specially noticed, because in Palestine for a large part of the year the grass is brown. And as we saw, in the story of Jesus stilling the storm, Mark (but not the other Gospels) includes the detail that He was asleep 'in the stern' of the boat, 'on the cushion' (Mark 4.38). As a fisherman, accustomed to working in boats, Peter might specially have noticed where Jesus was lying. (Perhaps it was Peter's boat.)

DETAILS IN THE GOSPEL STORIES

There are several reasons which the Gospel writers may have had for including details in their stories about Jesus:

1. The details may be an important part of the story itself; e.g. in the story of the woman with a flow of blood, the detail that she suffered for twelve years shows how severe her illness was (Mark 5.25).

2. The details may have a theological importance, e.g. in the story of Jesus feeding the 5,000 twelve baskets of food were picked up afterwards (Mark 6.30–44). These numbers may mean that Jesus fed Jews, because five and twelve are both significant numbers for Jews. In Mark's later story of Jesus feeding 4,000, when seven baskets of food were gathered up (Mark 8.1–10), the numbers may indicate that Gentiles too were fed, because seven was regarded as a symbol of completeness and four stood for the whole earth (see p. 96).

3. The details may have been received from eye-witnesses, who included them in the story because that was how they remembered it.

4. Some details may be added by the story-teller to give extra impact to the story. Most stories that are passed on orally include inessential details which the storyteller may add to, change, or leave out.

Almost certainly the evangelists included some details for more than one of these reasons. A detail may have been accurately remembered and *also* have a theological significance, e.g. John's Gospel records that Nicodemus, a ruler of the Jews, came to Jesus 'by night' (John 3.2). The writer may have included this detail as a theological symbol, to signify that Nicodemus came from the darkness of ignorance to Jesus, the Light of the world. And it may at the same time be a true remembrance of what really happened.

The view that the writer of Mark's Gospel was a close associate of Peter does not depend only on tradition. Mark records in great detail three occasions when Peter, James and John were the only disciples present with Jesus. This Gospel also gives us a specially vivid picture of Peter, recording a number of the foolish things that Peter said and did.

We shall see in chapter 7 that the association of Mark's Gospel with Peter was one reason why it came to be accepted as Scripture.

STUDY SUGGESTIONS

WORDS AND MEANINGS

1. Explain the meaning of 'text' in the phrase 'the Gospel texts'.
2. What is meant by the sentence 'Mark and Paul were reconciled later'?
3. Explain the meaning of the following words:
   (a) significant   (b) evidence

REVIEW OF CONTENT

4. Where in the Gospels do the names of their writers appear?
5. (a) With which early Church leader is Mark most often associated in the New Testament?
   (b) With which Church leader is Mark most often associated in the traditions of the Church?
6. Which Church honours Mark as its first Bishop?
7. For what *chief* reasons do you yourself think that the Gospel writers included incidental details such as the green grass (Mark 6.39) in their stories?

BIBLE STUDY

8. Read Mark 5.35–43; 9.2–13; 14.32–42.
   (a) Which of the disciples are recorded as being present on the occasions described?
   (b) Why do you think that the names of those particular disciples are recorded?
9. Say in each case what you think the writer's reasons were for including the following details in Mark's Gospel:
   (a) That when Jesus had healed Jairus's daughter *He told her parents to give her something to eat* (Mark 5.43).
   (b) That after Jesus had taught in the synagogue at Capernaum and healed Peter's mother-in-law, the people of the city brought their sick for Him to heal *that same evening at sundown* (Mark 1.32).
   (c) That when Peter and James and John saw Jesus transfigured on the mountain, *Moses and Elijah appeared to them and were talking with Jesus there* (Mark 9.4).
   (d) That when Jesus miraculously fed the 5,000, and again at the Last Supper, *after He had blessed the bread, He broke it* (Mark 6.41; and compare 8.6; 14.22).
10. Read Acts 13.13; 15.36–41.
    (a) What explanation is given for John Mark's leaving Paul and his companions?
    (b) How do we know that Mark continued his missionary activity after these events?

FURTHER STUDY AND DISCUSSION

11. What different things might Papias have meant when he said that Mark wrote down what he remembered, 'without however recording in order'?

12. There is a tradition that the young man who ran away naked from the Garden of Gethsemane (Mark 14.51–52) was Mark himself. What evidence is there if any, to support this tradition? Do you yourself accept it or reject it, and for what reasons? Why do you think the story about the young man was recorded?

13. (a) What sort of evidence should we look for, to support traditions about the founding of the Church?
(b) In which countries is it most likely that there will be good evidence for traditions about the founding of the Church there?

14. What traditions are there about the founders of the Church in your own country? What evidence, if any, is there, for the truth of those traditions? What value do you yourself place on tradition in general?

15. (a) How far do you think Mark's Gospel shows that the writer had first-hand knowledge of the character of Peter?
(b) How far do you think Mark's Gospel shows an understanding of the teaching of Paul?

A GOSPEL FOR GENTILES

EMPHASIS ON THE DEATH OF JESUS

In Mark's Gospel there is a strong emphasis on the death of Jesus. The Gospel starts with an account of the ministry of John the Baptist, and the baptism of Jesus. Soon after describing the beginning of Jesus's ministry Mark points ahead to His death: 'The Pharisees went out and immediately held counsel with the Herodians against him, how to destroy him' (Mark 3.6).

In Mark's record of Jesus' ministry a turning-point comes when Peter confesses, 'You are the Christ' (Mark 8.29). After that, Jesus 'began to teach them that the Son of man must suffer many things, and be rejected by the elders and the chief priests, and the scribes, and be killed, and after three days rise again' (Mark 8.31). From that time onwards Jesus constantly taught the disciples that He would have to suffer and die. A third of Mark's Gospel is given to the passion narrative. 'And they were on the road, going up to Jerusalem, and Jesus was walking ahead of them; and they were amazed, and those who followed were afraid. And taking the twelve again he began to tell them what was to happen to him, saying, "Behold, we are going up to Jerusalem; and the Son of man will be delivered to the chief priests and the scribes, and they will condemn him to death, and deliver him to the Gentiles; and they will mock him, and spit upon him, and scourge him, and kill him; and after three days he will rise" ' (Mark 10.32–34). For Mark the supremely important event was that Jesus suffered and died (see Vol. 1, ch. 4).

It seems strange that Mark does not include any detailed or vivid stories about the risen Jesus. The earliest versions we have of this Gospel end at Mark 16.8, with the words 'for they were afraid!' (verses 9–20 were added later, to make the ending less abrupt; see pp. 111 and 117 below). Biblical scholars disagree about the reason why the Gospel ended at 16.8. Some think that it was the writer's intention to end his account of Jesus' life with the story of the empty tomb. Others believe that the end is missing from the earliest surviving manuscripts. Perhaps the writer was prevented from completing his work, or he wrote an ending which was torn off and lost. The lack of stories in this Gospel about Jesus' birth and resurrection gives even more weight to the passion narrative.

URGENCY AND ACTION

Most of the material in Mark's Gospel is narrative, recording more of what Jesus *did* than of what He *said*. Story follows story, giving a sense of movement and urgency. Mark often begins a sentence or a paragraph with 'and', or even 'and immediately'. For example: '*And* they went into Capernaum; *and immediately* on the sabbath he entered the synagogue and taught. *And* they were astonished at the teaching, for he taught them as one who had authority, and not as the scribes. *And immediately* there was in their synagogue a man with an unclean spirit; *and* he cried out, "What have you to do with us, Jesus of Nazareth? Have you come to destroy us? I know who you are, the Holy One of God." ' (Mark 1.21–24).

This style of writing gives a sense of urgency to Mark's story of Jesus. It shows Jesus busy doing God's work, and hastening towards His death. The events which Mark records are set in the context of a single year, a year which was a time of decision: 'The time is fulfilled, and the kingdom of God is at hand; repent, and believe in the Gospel' (Mark 1.15).

TEACHING IN MARK'S GOSPEL

There is less of Jesus' teaching in Mark's Gospel than in the other three. Much of the teaching which Mark has included is concerned with the need for the Son of Man to suffer and die.

In Mark, Jesus' teaching is closely associated with events; e.g. after

His meeting with the rich young ruler Jesus taught His disciples about riches, and His teaching about marriage followed from a question which the Pharisees asked about divorce. In Mark 13 there is a block of teaching which is sometimes called 'the Little Apocalypse', or the 'eschatological discourse', in which Mark has gathered together Jesus' teaching about the end of the world and about His own return as judge. Except for that passage, the teaching recorded in Mark does not come in blocks such as we find in the other Gospels. Matthew and John contain whole chapters of words spoken by Jesus.

Matthew and Luke both record many of the stories which Jesus told. But Mark records only four of Jesus's story parables: three about seeds growing (Mark 4.1–32) and the parable of the wicked tenants (Mark 12.1–11).

VIVID DESCRIPTIONS

We have already seen that many of the stories in Mark are full of little details which the other Gospel writers have not included. Most of the miracle stories which we find in Matthew, Mark and Luke are longer in Mark. For example, the story of Jairus's daughter takes up nine verses in Matthew, seventeen verses in Luke, and twenty-three verses in Mark (Matt. 9.18–26; Luke 8.40–56; Mark 5.21–43).

More than any other Gospel writer Mark records the actual Aramaic words that Jesus spoke. Only Mark tells us that when Jesus raised Jairus's daughter He said, '*Talitha cumi*', and that when He healed a deaf man He said '*Ephphatha*' (Mark 5.41; 7.34).

PRONOUNCEMENT STORIES

Although many of the stories in Mark are told at length with a lot of detail, not all his stories are like that. Some are short, and contain very little detail (e.g. Mark 2.15–17). The reason why such stories were handed down in the Church was that they provided a framework for a saying of Jesus (see p. 14). Mark did not necessarily hear these 'pronouncement stories' from Peter. He would have received information about Jesus from other sources as well.

THE MYSTERY OF JESUS

'Who then is this, that even wind and sea obey him?' (Mark 4.41).

THE SON OF GOD

Mark wrote his Gospel in the firm belief that Jesus was the Messiah, and the Son of God. The opening words of his Gospel read, 'The beginning of the gospel of Jesus Christ the Son of God' (Mark 1.1). 'Son of God' in this verse may have been an editorial addition (see p. 4), but if so the editor accurately described the theme of the whole Gospel.

In two passages Mark describes a voice from heaven which announces that Jesus is 'my beloved son' (Mark 1.11; 9.7), and he tells of several occasions when people possessed by demons called Jesus the Son of God. Even the Roman centurion who stood by the cross called Him 'Son of God' (Mark 15.39).

Mark shows that this side of Jesus was mostly hidden. When unclean spirits recognized Him, Jesus commanded them to be silent. Often He told the people whom He had healed that they should not tell others, e.g. after healing a leper Jesus 'sternly charged him, and sent him away at once, and said to him, "See that you say nothing to anyone; but go, show yourself to the priest" (Mark 1.44).

Immediately after Jesus had encouraged Peter to acknowledge Him as the Messiah, He told him not to tell anyone else: 'and he asked them "But who do you say that I am?" Peter answered him, "You are the Christ." And he charged them to tell no one about him' (Mark 8.29–30).

Jesus's desire for secrecy about His true nature is one of the distinctive characteristics of Mark's Gospel. Mark records only one occasion when Jesus openly proclaimed Himself. That was at His trial: 'Again the high priest asked him, "Are you the Christ, the Son of the Blessed?" And Jesus said, "I am; and you will see the Son of man sitting at the right hand of Power, and coming with the clouds of heaven"' (Mark 14.61–62).

JESUS THE MAN

Many people clearly thought that Jesus was a prophet. 'Jesus asked his disciples, "Who do men say that I am?" And they told him, "John the Baptist; and others say, Elijah; and others one of the prophets"' (Mark 8.27–28). When Mark was writing the Gospel, he understood that Jesus was far greater than a prophet. However, he showed that during Jesus's lifetime even His disciples did not understand who He was. They knew Him as a man. Mark strongly emphasized the humanity of Jesus.

Mark gives us a picture of Jesus as a person who felt things deeply, and who showed His feelings. When He was with children He picked them up and held them in His arms, and He was indignant when the disciples tried to stop mothers from bringing their children to Him for a blessing (Mark 10.13–16). When the rich young ruler came to Him, 'Jesus looking upon him loved him' (Mark 10.21).

Jesus expressed anger and impatience. Often He became impatient with the disciples because of their lack of understanding. He was also annoyed by the attitude of some of the Pharisees: 'And they watched him to see whether he would heal him on the sabbath, so that they might accuse him . . . and he looked around at them with anger, grieved at their hardness of heart' (Mark 3.2–5).

Mark also recorded that Jesus' power was limited. In the story of the woman who had a flow of blood for twelve years, she touched Jesus' clothes and was healed. 'And Jesus, perceiving in himself that power had gone forth from him, immediately turned about in the crowd, and said, "Who touched me?" . . . And he looked around to see who had done it' (Mark 5.30–32). According to Mark Jesus knew that power had gone from Him, but He did not know who had touched Him, or why. In Matthew's version of the same story we read only that Jesus turned and saw her, and said, 'Take heart, daughter; your faith has made you well' (Matt. 9.22).

THE DISCIPLES' UNDERSTANDING OF JESUS

Mark showed the twelve to be men who had left their homes to follow Jesus, but who had very little understanding of who He really was. Even the three disciples who were closest to Jesus did not understand Him any better than the others. Peter could say 'You are the Christ', but he did not understand what sort of Messiah Jesus was. When Jesus began to tell them that He must suffer and die, Peter rebuked Him. James and John did not understand either; they went to Jesus and asked Him, 'Grant us to sit, one at your right hand and one at your left, in your glory' (Mark 10.37). They were expecting an earthly kingdom.

In Mark's story of Jesus calming the storm it seems that the disciples did not expect Jesus to save them. They were simply resentful because He was sleeping peacefully in the stern while they struggled with the boat in the storm. 'Teacher, do you not care if we perish?' they cried (Mark 4.38).

It is a characteristic of Mark's Gospel that the disciples only call Jesus 'Teacher'. In the other three Gospels the disciples are often described as addressing Him as 'Lord'. Mark himself believed that Jesus was Lord, but he did not think that the disciples really believed it until after the resurrection.

A GOSPEL FOR GENTILES

Jesus was a Jew who spent the whole of His ministry in Palestine among Jews. Mark was also a Jew, but the two cities with which he is traditionally associated are Rome and Alexandria. These were both Gentile cities. Both had large Jewish populations, but the majority of the Christians there were probably Gentiles. Mark was careful in his Gospel to explain Jewish customs for the sake of his Gentile readers. 'For the Pharisees and all the Jews do not eat unless they wash their hands' (Mark 7.3). He explained that '*corban*' means 'given to God', and that the day of Preparation is the day before the sabbath (Mark 7.11; 15.42).

When Mark wrote down Jesus' teaching about divorce, he expected

'Mark expected most of his readers to be Gentiles, and he wanted them to understand the real significance of Jesus' teaching.' This is one reason why some present-day missionaries find Mark's Gospel the most suitable for introducing new Christians to the faith—like this young Pakistani lay worker on a round of house-to-house visiting.

that most of his readers would be Gentiles. Among the Jews a man could divorce his wife, but a woman could not divorce her husband; but under the Roman law a woman *could* divorce her husband. According to Matthew and Luke, Jesus' teaching about divorce was only concerned with men who divorced their wives, or who married divorced women. That is what we would expect, since Jesus was a Jew speaking to Jews. But Mark was concerned that his readers should understand the real significance of Jesus' teaching: that divorce is wrong for everyone: 'Whoever divorces his wife and marries another, commits adultery against her; and if she divorces her husband and marries another, she commits adultery' (Mark 10.11–12).

STUDY SUGGESTIONS

WORDS AND MEANINGS

1. Explain the meaning of the following words as used in this chapter:
   (a) emphasis   (b) characteristic

REVIEW OF CONTENT

2. What proportion of Mark's Gospel is given to the passion narrative?
3. When the same story occurs in Matthew, Mark and Luke, which version is usually the longest?
4. How did the disciples address Jesus, according to Mark?
5. (a) What words and phrases used often in Mark's Gospel give it a feel of urgency?
   (b) Write out the remainder of the story about the man with the unclean spirit, and about Peter's mother-in-law (Mark 1.25–31), and underline all the words and phrases of this sort that you can find in it.
6. (a) What did Mark's use of Aramaic phrases add to his Gospel?
   (b) Why did he need to give Greek translations of the Aramaic words?

BIBLE STUDY

7. Read Mark 6.1–6 and Matt. 13.53–58.
   (a) In what way does Mark show that Jesus' power was limited when He visited 'his own country'?
   (b) In what way is Matthew's account different from Mark's?
8. Read Mark 8.14–21. How would you describe the way Jesus felt when He said, 'Do you not yet understand?' (v. 21)?
9. Read Mark 9.2–8 and 14.32–42. What do you learn about Peter, James and John from these passages?

FURTHER STUDY AND DISCUSSION

10. 'And he charged them to tell no one about him' (Mark 8.30). Mark repeatedly describes Jesus as wanting to keep secret that He was the Messiah.

(a) For what reasons do you think Jesus wanted to keep His true nature secret?

(b) How far do you think it is right for Christians today to keep their faith a secret?

11. Matthew, Mark and Luke and Paul record slightly different teaching by Jesus on the subject of divorce (see Matt. 5.32: Mark 10.11; Luke 16.18; 1 Cor. 7.10–11).

(a) How can you explain the differences?

(b) What do you think should be the Church's attitude today towards those who are divorced?

12. Christian theologians have always insisted that Jesus was fully man and fully God. Why? What reply would you give to someone who told you, 'I can accept Jesus as a prophet and a teacher, but not as the Son of God'?

3

The Gospel According to Matthew

AUTHORSHIP: A CONCERN FOR THE LAW

Tradition has always associated Matthew's Gospel with Matthew the tax collector, who was one of the Twelve.

MATTHEW IN THE NEW TESTAMENT

'As Jesus passed on from there, he saw a man called Matthew sitting at the tax office; and he said to him, "Follow me." And he rose and followed him' (Matt. 9.9).

Matthew's Gospel contains this short account of Jesus calling Matthew the tax-collector to be a disciple. Mark and Luke tell the same story but call the tax-collector 'Levi' (Mark 2.13–14; Luke 5.25–28). From this we deduce that Matthew and Levi are two names for the same person. All three Gospels record that many 'tax-collectors and sinners' gathered later at the tax-collector's house to meet Jesus. According to Luke's account 'Levi made him a great feast'. The Pharisees criticized Jesus for eating and drinking with sinners.

Apart from this story, and Matthew's name in the lists of the Twelve (Matt. 10.2–4; Mark 3.16–19; Luke 6.13–16; Acts 1.13) we have no other New Testament information about him. All the lists call him Matthew, and make no mention of Levi.

MATTHEW IN THE TRADITION OF THE CHURCH

According to the fourth-century Church historian, Eusebius, Matthew preached to the Hebrews. In the second century Papias wrote, 'Matthew compiled the sayings in the Hebrew language and each one interpreted them as best he could.' Probably Papias was not referring to our Gospel of Matthew. The scholars all agree that Matthew's Gospel was written in Greek, and Papias stated that Matthew compiled 'the sayings'. Matthew's Gospel is far more than a mere collection of sayings. Papias may have meant that Matthew the apostle made a collection of the sayings of Jesus. Another widely-held theory is that Matthew was responsible for a collection of proof texts from the Hebrew Scriptures, which each teacher in the early Church then interpreted 'as best he could' (see p. 3).

THE AUTHOR OF MATTHEW'S GOSPEL

We have noticed that many of the stories in Matthew can also be found in Mark and Luke, and we have seen some of the reasons for thinking that Matthew and Luke both used a version of Mark when they wrote their Gospels. Luke had not known Jesus during His life on earth, so he did need to get his information about Jesus from other people. But if Matthew the apostle had written the first Gospel, he would surely have had no need to use Mark, because he would have had his own memories of Jesus.

We have no way of knowing who wrote this Gospel. The apostle Matthew may have inspired someone else to write it. Possibly it began with a collection of proof texts which the apostle made. The exact connection between Matthew the apostle and the Gospel of Matthew remains a mystery. We can only say that this Gospel has always been associated with Matthew. Because of this association it was thought that the Gospel had been written first, and it was placed first in the New Testament (but see pp. 15–16).

A TIDY ARRANGEMENT

The study of Matthew's Gospel suggests that it developed over a long period of time. Scholars have found some evidence in this Gospel that it was written very early, and other evidence that it was written very late. Perhaps it was the earliest Gospel to be begun, and the last to be completed. If that is so, it probably went through many stages before it became the Gospel that we have in the Bible.

Perhaps it began with Matthew's collecting together Old Testament proof texts in Hebrew, and writing them down. As the Church spread, and needed to have proof texts in Greek, so the Greek version of the Scriptures would have been used instead. Incidents in Jesus's life may have been collected and written down, alongside the Old Testament texts. Perhaps more and more sayings of Jesus and stories about Him were added. The person who finally edited all this material to make the Gospel as we know it arranged it in a very orderly way. One of the reasons why Matthew's Gospel has always been popular is the tidy way in which the sayings and stories are arranged (see p. 37). Perhaps this tidy way of doing things, and the concern for the law which appears throughout this Gospel, support the traditional association with Matthew the tax-collector, a 'civil servant' accustomed to interpreting rules and regulations!

Although we do not know the name of the final writer it is convenient to call him 'Matthew', as Christians have done for centuries.

A GOSPEL FOR JEWISH CHRISTIANS

THE PLAN OF THIS GOSPEL

The material in Matthew's Gospel has been very carefully sorted out, and organized into blocks, as the diagram below shows. In particular we may notice two things about the plan.

PLAN OF MATTHEW'S GOSPEL

Narrative	Teaching
Matt. 1.1—2.23 The coming of Jesus as Messiah: Stories about Jesus' birth	
Matt. 3.1—4.25 Jesus' ministry begins in Galilee	
	Matt. 5.1—7.29 The Sermon on the Mount
Matt. 8.1—9.35 Nine miracles showing Jesus as the Messiah	
	Matt. 9.36—10.42 Instructions to missionaries
Matt. 11.1—12.50 Jesus' relationship with: (a) John the Baptist, (b) the Pharisees	
	Matt. 13.1—52 Seven parables of the Kingdom
Matt. 13.53—17.27 Jesus' ministry in Galilee	
	Matt. 18.1—35 Teaching about Christian life, and especially about forgiveness
Matt. 19.1—22.46 Going up to Jerusalem	
	Matt. 23.1—25.46 Sayings about Scribes and Pharisees Teaching about the last things
Matt. 26–1—28.20 The Passion Story: Jesus' suffering, death and resurrection	

---

1. FIVE BLOCKS OF TEACHING

Mark and Luke linked the teaching of Jesus with the narrative about Him in their Gospels, but this is not so in Matthew's Gospel. The teaching has been carefully arranged according to subjects, and divided into five 'books', which are often called 'discourses'. Scholars think that the writer may have intended them to be five new law books to replace the five law books of Moses.

The first 'book' of teaching begins with the words, 'He went up on the mountain' (Matt. 5.1). Just as the old law of Moses was given on a mountain, so was the new law of Jesus. This first collection of sayings, which has come to be called the Sermon on the Mount, is mostly concerned with the law of Moses, and with Jesus's reinterpretation of it: 'Think not that I have come to abolish the law and the prophets; I have come not to abolish them but to fulfil them' (Matt. 5.17). 'You have heard that it was said, "You shall love your neighbour and hate your enemy." But I say to you, love your enemies and pray for those who persecute you, so that you may be sons of your Father who is in heaven' (Matt. 5.43–45).

2. A STRUCTURED NARRATIVE

Matthew arranged his material according to subject matter, and not necessarily in the order in which events happened. The broad outline of events is the same as in Mark and Luke, but individual stories appear in a different order. For example, Matthew gathered together stories which show Jesus' relationship with the Pharisees. He also collected nine stories about Jesus performing miracles. These nine miracles are not merely told one after another, they are organized into three groups to show the special nature of Jesus' power:

Group 1. *Three Healings of despised people*
  Matt. 8.1–4, a leper,
  Matt. 8.5–13, a Gentile's servant,
  Matt. 8.14–17, a woman; Peter's mother-in-law.
Group 2. *Three Signs of Power*
  Matt. 8.23–27, Stilling the storm,
  Matt. 8.28–34, Casting out demons,
  Matt. 9.1–8, Pardoning and healing a paralysed man.
Group 3. *Three Double Healings*
  Matt. 9.18–26, Jairus's daughter and the woman with the flow of blood,
  Matt. 9.27–31, Two blind men,
  Matt. 9.32–34 A man who was dumb and demon-possessed.

JESUS AND THE JEWISH LAW

Matthew's Gospel is full of references to Judaism, and to current Jewish practices, but the author does not explain Jewish terms in the way that Mark does. Probably the Christians he was writing for were mostly Jewish Christians.

Matthew was concerned to show Jesus as a true Jew. He opens the

Gospel with a genealogy, or 'family tree', in which he traces Jesus' ancestors, and shows how He was descended from Abraham and David (Matt. 1.2,6). Luke on the other hand, traces Jesus' descent back to Adam, the father of *all* human beings.

In the Sermon on the Mount Matthew shows Jesus as a Messiah who came not to destroy the old law, but to fulfil it. He shows that Jesus accepted the authority of the law of Moses: 'Whoever then relaxes one of the least of these commandments and teaches men so, shall be called least in the kingdom of heaven; but he who does them and teaches them shall be called great in the kingdom of heaven' (Matt. 5.19). Jesus did not criticize the law itself, but the common Jewish interpretation of the law. According to Matthew 23.1–39 Jesus attacked the failings of some of the scribes and the Pharisees, who oppressed the people and 'neglected the law, justice, mercy and faith'.

All through Matthew's Gospel the writer emphasizes the fulfilment of the Old Testament. This Gospel contains over 130 references to the Old Testament, more than any of the other Gospels. The birth stories especially are full of Old Testament prophecies, introduced with words like these: 'This was to fulfil what the Lord had spoken by the prophet' (Matt. 2.15).

Matthew saw Jesus as the longed-for Messiah, and did not hide His royal status. In this Gospel Jesus is called 'Son of David' eight times. According to Matthew, Jesus at the time of His arrest thought of Himself as a royal prince: 'Do you think that I cannot appeal to my Father, and he will at once send me more than twelve legions of angels? But how then should the scriptures be fulfilled, that it must be so?' (Matt. 26.53–54).

In Matthew's account of the mission of the Twelve, Jesus instructs His disciples not to go to the Gentiles or to the Samaritans (Matt. 10.5–6). By including this detail Matthew emphasized something which all the evangelists accepted, that the mission to the Gentiles belonged to the period after the crucifixion.

A CONCERN FOR ALL THE WORLD

Although the writer of this Gospel had a strong Jewish interest, he also recognized that Jesus was not just a Messiah for the Jews. Jesus was for *everyone*. In the nine miracles that Matthew gathered together to show Jesus as the Messiah, the first three are about His healing people who were despised by Jews: a leper, a woman, and a Roman centurion's servant. Other miracles are then shown as fulfilling a prophecy of Isaiah:

'Behold my servant whom I have chosen,
My beloved with whom my soul is well pleased.
I will put my spirit upon him,

'Matthew emphasized the fulfilment of the Old Testament in Jesus, and many artists and sculptors have illustrated this theme, as in this early mosaic in Naples. It shows Jesus giving His New Covenant to Peter. Matthew's 'deep concern for Church structures and discipline' is especially interesting to people in training – like these Mexican students – for service in ministry and mission.

And he shall proclaim justice to the Gentiles.
... in his name will the Gentiles hope.'
(Matt. 12.18–21, cf. Isa. 42–4)
At the beginning of the Gospel Matthew tells of the wise men – Gentiles – coming to worship Jesus. He ends with the risen Jesus commanding His disciples, 'Go therefore and make disciples of all nations, baptizing them in the name of the Father and of the Son and of the Holy Spirit, teaching them to observe all that I have commanded you' (Matt. 28.19).

A CONCERN FOR THE CHURCH

Matthew shows the Church as the new Israel. Just as the old Israel had twelve tribes, so the new Israel has twelve disciples, who will sit on twelve thrones on the day of judgement (Matt. 19.28).

This Gospel shows a concern with Church structures and organization which we do not find in the other Gospels. Only Matthew records Jesus' saying to Peter, 'You are Peter, and on this rock I will build my Church' (Matt. 16.18). Only Matthew includes instructions by Jesus about what to do if a fellow Christian has sinned against you, and will not listen to you: 'If he does not listen, take one or two others along with you, that every word may be confirmed by the evidence of two or three witnesses. If he refuses to listen to them, tell it to the church; and if he refuses to listen to the church, let him be to you as a Gentile and a tax-collector' (Matt. 18.16–17). This is the only Gospel in which Jesus is described as using the word 'church'.

A TENDENCY TO LEGISLATE

The instruction about what to do when a fellow Christian sins against us shows a movement towards making rules and regulations. We have also noticed a concern for law in the Sermon on the Mount (Matt. 5.19).

There is a difference between the instructions given in Matthew about a sinning brother and the parallel passage in Luke (Matt. 18.15–17; Luke 17.3–4). Matthew and Luke both record Jesus' teaching that we have to forgive our brother, but in Luke's version there is no mention of what to do if our brother does not repent. Jesus' teaching about divorce as recorded in Matthew seems to show the same legalizing trend (Matt. 19.9; cf. Mark 10.11; Luke 16.18).

Scholars regard this tendency to make rules, and the concern about the Church, as evidence that Matthew was written at a fairly late date.

MATTHEW'S UNDERSTANDING OF JESUS AND HIS DISCIPLES

Matthew's picture of Jesus is more respectful and dignified than the one we find in Mark. In Matthew's account the disciples usually address

Jesus as 'Lord'. Stories about Jesus in this Gospel include much less detail, and do not refer to Jesus as being angry or sad or indignant. Where Mark writes of Jesus taking a child in His arms, Matthew has only, 'he put him in the midst of them' (Matt. 18.2). Some passages in Matthew include details which emphasize Jesus' *power*: He heals *two* madmen at Gadara, and *two* blind men in Jericho (Matt. 8.28–34; 20.29–34). When He curses the fig tree, it withers *immediately* (Matt. 21.19).

Matthew's picture of the disciples shows them as having more understanding of Jesus and His mission than they appear to have in Mark. According to Matthew when Jesus told the parables of the Kingdom, He then asked His disciples, 'Have you understood all this?' and they answered, 'Yes' (Matt. 13.51).

Matthew also gives specially great honour to Peter. Only this Gospel includes the story of Peter walking on the water (Matt. 14.28–33), and records Jesus' promise to him, 'I will give you the keys of the kingdom of heaven, and whatever you loose on earth shall be loosed in heaven' (Matt. 16.19).

A CONCERN FOR JUDGEMENT AND THE LAST THINGS

All four Gospels record Jesus' teaching that He would return in power and glory at the Last Judgement, but Matthew shows a special interest in those final events. The Little Apocalypse found in Mark 13 is expanded in Matthew 24. In Matthew 24.51 and in five other passages we find the expression, 'and men will weep and gnash their teeth'. This expression appears once in Luke, and not at all in Mark and John.

Matthew is the only Gospel writer to use the word '*parousia*' to mean the second coming of Jesus, and he seems to have expected that the return of Jesus would happen in the near future: 'Truly, I say to you, there are some standing here who will not taste death before they see the Son of man coming in his kingdom' (Matt. 16.28; cf. 10.23; 24.34). This expectation points to an early date for the Gospel, in contrast to the later date which is suggested by the concern for rules and regulations, and for the Church (see p. 41).

Many of the parables in this Gospel are about the end of the world, and the judgement that will come upon us. There will be a harvest time, a time of gathering in (Matt. 13.24–30, 47–50), a time of reckoning (Matt. 20.8; 24.50; 24.19), a time when the Son of man will separate the sheep from the goats (Matt. 25.31–46). Matthew includes several parables about the need to be ready and waiting, because no one, not even the Son Himself, knows when the final time will be, e.g. the faithful servant, and the wise and foolish maidens (Matt. 24.45–51; 25.1–13).

MATERIAL FOUND ONLY IN MATTHEW

The following is a brief outline of the material which appears only in Matthew, and not in the other Gospels.

NARRATIVE

Jesus' family tree, as far back as Abraham (Matt. 1.1–17).
The angel appearing to Joseph in a dream (Matt. 1.18–25).
Visit of the wise men (Matt. 2.1–12).
Joseph warned in a dream to flee to Egypt (Matt. 2.13–15).
Herod's massacre of the children (Matt. 2.16–18).
Joseph, Mary and Jesus return to live in Nazareth (Matt. 2.19–23).
John the Baptist's reluctance to baptize Jesus (Matt. 3.14–15).
Peter walking on the water (Matt. 14.29–31).
Peter, the foundation of the Church (Matt. 16.17–19).
The shekel in the fish's mouth (Matt. 17.24–27).
Jesus healing in the Temple (Matt. 21.14–17).
The fate of Judas (Matt. 27.3–10).
Pilate's wife's warning (Matt. 27.19).
The opening of the tombs (Matt. 27.52–53).
The guard at the tomb (Matt. 27.62–66).
The guards bribed (Matt. 28.11–17).
Jesus' appearance on a mountain in Galilee (Matt. 28.16–20).

PARABLES

The wheat and the weeds (Matt. 13.24–30).
The treasure in the field (Matt. 13.44).
The pearl of great value (Matt. 13.45–46).
The householder (Matt. 13.51–52).
The unforgiving servant (Matt. 18.23–35).
The labourers in the vineyard (Matt. 20.1–16).
Two sons (Matt. 21.28–31).
The wedding garment (Matt. 22.1–14).
Ten maidens (Matt. 25.1–13).
The sheep and the goats (Matt. 25.31–46).

OTHER TEACHING

Some of the Beatitudes, or 'blessings' (in Matt. 5.1–12).
The place of the law (Matt. 5.19–20).
The need to be reconciled with our fellow Christians (Matt. 5.21–24).
Looking at a woman with lust (Matt. 5.27–30).
Divorce and adultery (Matt. 5.31–32).
Swearing (Matt. 5.33–37).
Prayer (Matt. 6.5–8).
Fasting (Matt. 6.16–18).

Almsgiving (Matt. 6.2–4).
Don't give dogs what is holy (Matt. 7.6).
John the Baptist is Elijah returned (Matt. 11.14–15).
'Come to me all who labour and are heavy laden' (Matt. 11.28–30).
Jesus is greater than the Temple (Matt. 12.5–7).
Marriage and celibacy (Matt. 19.10–12).
Some of the criticisms of the scribes and Pharisees (e.g. Matt. 23.2–5).

STUDY SUGGESTIONS

WORDS AND MEANINGS

1. Explain the meaning of the following words:
   (a) genealogy   (b) discourse   (c) beatitudes
2. Explain the phrase 'A Tendency to Legislate' (p. 41).

REVIEW OF CONTENT

3. For what reason(s) do scholars think that Matthew and Levi were probably the same man?
4. Do the following statements give a true account of the evidence? Give reasons for your answer in each case.
   (a) Matthew the apostle has always been associated with the first Gospel.
   (b) Eusebius said that Matthew preached to the Hebrews.
   (c) Papias said that Matthew wrote a Gospel in Hebrew.
5. (a) How many 'blocks' of teaching are there in Matthew?
   (b) What is the possible significance of that number?
6. What evidence is there in Matthew's Gospel that it was written mainly for Jewish Christians?
7. Give at least one reason for the popularity of Matthew's Gospel.
8. Give examples of material recorded only in Matthew's Gospel relating to Jesus'
   (a) teaching   (b) actions   (c) passion (i.e. suffering and death)

BIBLE STUDY

9. (a) Give an example of a verse in Matthew's Gospel which appears to have been written very soon after Jesus's death, and explain why you have chosen it.
   (b) Give an example of a verse which appears to have been written later on, and explain why you have chosen it.
10. Read Matt. 8.23–27 and Mark 4.35–41. What differences do you find between Matthew's account of Jesus stilling the storm, and Mark's account? In what way does Matthew's account give us a different picture of the disciples?

11. Read the promise of Jesus to the disciples in Matt. 19.28. To whom did the writer think the promise referred? Compare this passage with 1 Cor. 6.2. Who did Paul think was going to judge the world?

FURTHER STUDY AND DISCUSSION

12. What connection do you consider there may be between our understanding that Matthew's is a very Jewish Gospel, and the harsh words of Jesus about scribes and Pharisees which it records?
13. All the Gospel writers contribute to the picture we have of Jesus. What would you regard as being Matthew's special contribution?
14. The material in Matthew's Gospel has been carefully arranged according to a tidy plan. In what ways are tidiness and good organization helpful—or unhelpful—in the preaching of the gospel?

4
Luke–Acts: A Book in Two Parts

'It seemed good to me also, having followed all things closely for some time past, to write an orderly account for you, most excellent Theophilus' (Luke 1.3)

AUTHORSHIP: A CONCERN FOR HISTORY

From earliest times Christians have believed that the writer of Luke's Gospel and of the Acts of the Apostles was Luke, a doctor and a companion of Paul. His name appears three times in the New Testament. In Colossians Paul sends greetings from 'Luke the beloved physician and Demas' (Col. 4.14), and the letter to Philemon also includes greetings from Luke (Philemon 24); in 2 Timothy 4.11 we read 'Luke alone is with me'.

Luke may have been a Gentile. In Colossians he is not included among 'the men of the circumcision' (Col. 4.10–11). Certainly the writer of Luke's Gospel makes no claim to have been an eyewitness of the events of Jesus' life. He states that 'they were delivered to us by those who from the beginning were eye-witnesses'. The author's only claim is that he had 'followed all things closely for some time past' (Luke 1.2–3).

TWO VOLUMES

The author of Luke's Gospel not only wrote an account of the life, death and resurrection of Jesus. He also wrote an account of the birth and work of the Church, the book which we call the Acts of the Apostles. The introduction to Luke's Gospel is really an introduction to both the Gospel and the Acts of the Apostles. If we look at the introduction to Acts alongside the introduction to the Gospel we see clearly that the Acts of the Apostles is the second volume.

'Inasmuch as many have undertaken to compile a narrative of the things which have been accomplished among us, just as they were delivered to us by those who from the beginning were eye-witnesses and ministers of the word, it seemed good to me also, having followed all things closely for some time past, to write an orderly account for you, most excellent Theophilus, that you may know the truth concerning the things of which you have been informed' (Luke 1.1–4).

'In the first book, O Theophilus, I have dealt with all that Jesus began to do and teach, until the day when he was taken up, after he had

46

given commandment through the Holy Spirit to the apostles whom he had chosen' (Acts 1.1–2).

'MOST EXCELLENT THEOPHILUS'

No one knows who Theophilus was. The literal meaning of the name is 'Lover of God'. Perhaps he was a high-born Roman official. Maybe he was someone who had expressed an interest in Christianity. Luke may have addressed his Gospel to Theophilus as a representative of the Roman world. In his Gospel and in the Acts of the Apostles Luke shows a greater concern than any other Gospel writer to present Jesus as a man in history, and the Church as a growing force in the world of his time. Certainly Luke took care to show Christianity as a world religion. He mentions two Roman Emperors, Tiberius and Augustus, and he dates the beginning of John the Baptist's ministry according to Roman dates: 'in the first year of Tiberius Caesar, Pontius Pilate being governor of Judaea' (Luke 3.1). In Luke's account of Jesus's trial, Pontius Pilate declares Jesus innocent three times, and the blame is put firmly on the Jews: 'They were urgent, demanding with loud cries that He should be crucified. And their voices prevailed' (Luke 23.23).

In the Acts of the Apostles Roman officials are generally shown as friendly and just men. According to Luke's account of the Church it was usually the Jews who stirred up trouble for the Christians.

In both books the details which Luke gives of dates and places help to authenticate his account, and in Acts alone he records almost 100 personal names.

THE GOSPEL ACCORDING TO LUKE

A GOSPEL FOR ALL PEOPLES

In the first part of his book – the Gospel – Luke records what God had done, beginning with the announcement of the birth of John the Baptist and ending with Jesus' ascension.

THE PLAN OF THIS GOSPEL

The plan of Luke's Gospel is very different from that of Matthew's tidy structure according to subject matter. If we read through the passages in Luke that are listed in the left-hand column of the diagram on p. 48, and leave out those that are listed in the right-hand column, we find that we are reading a continuous narrative. Luke 3.1–2 sounds like a beginning, an introduction, and the story of Jesus reads on smoothly from there. Mark had begun his Gospel with the story of John the

PLAN OF LUKE'S GOSPEL

Luke 3.1—4.30 John the Baptist and the baptism of Jesus A family tree, beginning with Adam The beginning of Jesus' ministry	*Luke 1.1—2.52* Stories about Jesus' birth
Luke 6.17—49 The Sermon on the Plain	*Luke 4.31—6.16* Stories about Jesus, (very like Mark)
Luke 7.1—8.3 Jesus' ministry in Galilee (stories from 'Q' & 'L')	*Luke 8.4—9.50* Stories about Jesus,
Luke 9.51—18.14 Jesus moving towards Jerusalem (stories from 'Q' and 'L')	(very like Mark)
Luke 19.1—24.53 The Passion Narrative (Partly like Mark; many stories found only in Luke)	*Luke 18.15—43* Stories about Jesus, (very like Mark)

Baptist, and it was a natural point at which to begin an account of Jesus' ministry.

PROTO-LUKE?

The arrangement of the material in Luke's Gospel has led many scholars to believe that Luke wrote an earlier edition, which they call 'Proto-Luke' ('*proto*' in Greek means 'first'). The content of Proto-Luke, if it existed, was all those passages listed in the left-hand column of the plan of Luke's Gospel. The theory is that Luke later added those in the right-hand column to his first edition:

(a) The birth stories. These form a prologue. The birth stories in Luke are different from the birth stories in Matthew. Luke's stories include a number of hymns, and seem to be written mainly from Mary's point of view. Possibly Luke did not know these stories when he wrote his first edition, or if he did know them, it was only later that he decided to use them.

(b) Extracts from Mark's Gospel, possibly an earlier edition of

48

Mark. Having compiled his own Gospel, Luke came to know the Gospel that Mark was writing (see p. 16), and inserted passages from it into his own. Three blocks of material in Luke are very like parts of Mark. These appear in the right-hand column of our plan, but it is also true that half of Mark does not appear at all in Luke. If Luke used an early edition of Mark it would help to explain these facts.

A HISTORICAL APPROACH

We have already noticed the references to Roman Emperors, which are part of Luke's system of dating (see Vol. 1, pp. 28–29). The other Gospel writers did not give dates for any of the events in Jesus's life, though Matthew put Jesus into a historical context by stating that He was born 'in the days of Herod the King' and that Joseph and Mary returned from Egypt when 'Archelaus reigned over Judaea in place of his father Herod' (Matt. 2.1,22). Luke, however, gave as clear a date as he could for the beginning of John the Baptist's ministry: 'In the fifteenth year of the reign of Tiberius Caesar, Pontius Pilate being governor of Judaea and Herod being tetrarch of Galilee, and his brother Philip tetrarch of the region of Ituraea and Trachonitis, and Lysanius tetrarch of Abilene, in the high priesthood of Annas and Caiaphas, the word of God came to John the son of Zechariah in the wilderness (Luke 3.1–2).

The birth stories in Luke are full of details about the time when things happened. Zechariah was a priest 'in the days of Herod, king of Judaea' (Luke 1.5). When Caesar Augustus ordered that a census should be taken, 'this was the first enrolment, when Quirinius was governor of Syria' (Luke 2.2). After the birth of Jesus, 'at the end of eight days, when he was circumcised, he was called Jesus' (Luke 2.21). Luke also liked to say how old people were. Anna the prophetess was eighty-four when Jesus was presented at the Temple (see Luke 2.36); Jesus was twelve years old when he went up to Jerusalem with His parents for the Passover (Luke 2.42); 'Jesus, when he began his ministry, was about thirty years of age' (Luke 3.23).

Details such as these were important to Luke because they emphasized the reliability of the traditions he was recording. Events which could be clearly dated were events which had really happened. Luke had set himself the job of writing 'an orderly account' and in part at least this meant a historical order. Even the way in which Luke introduces the stories of Jesus demonstrates this point. Where Mark has 'and', 'and immediately', or 'again', Luke has 'after this', 'while', 'when'.

Luke's Gospel comes the nearest to being a biography of Jesus, and is the only one which includes a story about Jesus when He was a boy (Luke 2.41–51).

A GEOGRAPHICAL APPROACH

In Luke's account of Jesus he wanted to show Jesus moving towards Jerusalem, and His ministry reaching its climax there: 'He set his face to go to Jerusalem' (Luke 9.51). The idea of Jesus 'going up to Jerusalem' is repeated often. 'He went on his way through towns and villages, teaching, and journeying towards Jerusalem' (Luke 14.22). 'He was near to Jerusalem' (Luke 19.11). 'He went on ahead, going up to Jerusalem' (Luke 19.28).

Probably Jesus visited Jerusalem several times during His ministry, but Luke does not mention any actual visit other than His final one. In Luke 10.38–42 we read that Jesus stayed in the home of Martha and Mary in Bethany. Bethany was less than two miles from Jerusalem, and Jesus was probably visiting the city at the time. But Luke does not mention such a visit, as it would have distracted attention from his wider theme.

Luke follows a similar geographical approach in Acts, the second volume of his book, where he shows how Jesus was proclaimed from Jerusalem to Rome.

A UNIVERSAL APPROACH

The good news about Jesus is for all the world. This is the message throughout the New Testament. Matthew and Luke both ended their Gospels in the same way, with Jesus' words to His disciples about preaching the gospel to all nations: 'Repentance and forgiveness of sins should be preached to all nations' (Luke 24.47, cf. Matt. 28.19). Luke took care to emphasize this theme throughout his Gospel

Strict Jews, such as the Pharisees, kept themselves apart from people whom they considered 'unclean'. This included all Gentiles, the Jews who collected taxes for the Romans, Samaritans, and prostitutes. But they could not avoid these people completely. They were ruled by the Romans, they had to pay their taxes, and sometimes they needed to travel through Samaria. However, the Pharisees avoided close physical contact. They would not enter the house of an 'unclean' person, and they would never eat with a tax collector or a Gentile. As well as these groups of 'unclean' people, Jewish rabbis tended to despise women in general.

All the records of Jesus' life make it clear that His attitude was in complete contrast to the usual Jewish attitude. He entered the houses of 'sinners'. He ate with them, and he showed love and concern for them. Luke emphasized this side of Jesus even more than the other Gospel writers did. He had a deep concern to show that 'the Son of man came to seek and save the lost' (Luke 19.10). In order to show that Jesus was a saviour for all peoples, and not only the Jews, Luke traced His ancestry back to Adam (Luke 3.23–38).

'Luke took care to show Christianity as a world religion, and ended his Gospel with the words of Jesus: "Repentance and forgiveness should be preached to all nations." ' We hear much today about the influence of television and radio in spreading the gospel, especially in North America. But some people think the appeal of 'world' evangelists like Billy Graham, preaching in person to meetings in one country after another, as here in Australia, has a more lasting influence. So too, perhaps, has the power of the printed word for people to study at leisure, like these bookstall-browsers in North India.

LUKE'S UNDERSTANDING OF JESUS

FRIEND OF TAX-COLLECTORS AND SINNERS

Luke emphasized Jesus' friendship with sinners even more strongly than the other Gospel writers did. A number of the stories showing this are found only in Luke's Gospel. Only Luke has the story of Zacchaeus, the tax collector who climbed up into a tree in order to see Jesus. The murmuring of the onlookers when Jesus told Zacchaeus 'I must stay at your house today' shows how unusual Jesus's action was (Luke 19.1–10). Another story which Luke included was about the prostitute who came to the house where Jesus was having a meal, washed His feet with her tears, and dried them with her hair. Again Luke tells of the amazement of the onlookers: 'If this man were a prophet he would have known who and what sort of woman this is who is touching him, for she is a sinner.' Jesus' response was to tell the woman, 'Your sins are forgiven' (Luke 7.36–50).

Some of Jesus' parables which appear only in Luke show His similar concern for the lost and despised: e.g. the lost coin, the prodigal son, the Pharisee and the tax-collector (Luke 15.8–10; 15.11–32; 18.9–14).

FRIEND OF SAMARITANS

The Jews had a deep hatred for Samaritans (see Vol. 1, p. 24). Jews considered that the Samaritan religion was corrupt, and that they were little better than heathen. A Jewish king had destroyed the Samaritan temple on Mount Gerizim about 125 years before Jesus was born, so it is not surprising that the Samaritans also hated the Jews.

Only John and Luke tell us about Jesus' attitude towards Samaritans. John recorded a meeting between Jesus and a Samaritan woman which resulted in a number of Samaritans becoming disciples. Luke included two stories which showed Jesus' acceptance of Samaritans, as well as the parable of the Good Samaritan (Luke 9.52–55; 17.11–19; 10.25–37).

FRIEND OF WOMEN

Jews considered that women were greatly inferior to men. There was a prayer which Jewish men said, thanking God that they were neither Gentiles, nor slaves, nor women. Jewish women were forbidden to study the law, and rabbis were especially careful to avoid women.

Jesus' attitude to women was very difficult from that of other rabbis. All the Gospel writers show that Jesus had dealings with women, but Luke records the most stories about the women in Jesus' life. Only Luke includes an account of the women disciples: 'The twelve were with him, and also some women' (Luke 8.1–2). Luke tells of Jesus staying in the home of Martha and Mary (Luke 10.38–42). Even Luke's stories about the birth of Jesus are told more from the point of view of Mary than of Joseph; and he has the story of the angel appearing to Mary, and Mary's visit to Elizabeth. Twice he states that Mary 'kept all these things in her heart' (Luke 2.19,51). Here is a list of the women whom we read about only in Luke's Gospel:

Elizabeth, mother of John the Baptist (Luke 1.5–60).
Anna the prophetess (Luke 2.36–38).
The widow at Nain (Luke 7.11–17).
The repentant prostitute (Luke 7.36–50).
The women disciples (Luke 8.2–3).
A woman who cried out that Jesus' mother was blessed (Luke 11.27–28).
A bent woman healed on the sabbath (Luke 13.10–17).
The weeping women following the cross (Luke 23.27–31).

Two parables about women are also found only in Luke:
The lost coin (Luke 15.8–10).
The widow and the judge (Luke 18.1–8).

THE LORDSHIP OF JESUS

Luke was specially concerned to show that Jesus was the *Lord*. The Greek word '*kurios*' meant a ruler, someone with authority. In the Greek translation of the Old Testament '*Kurios*' was used as a title for God. Some pagans addressed their gods as 'Lord', and it could also mean 'Master', or simply 'Sir'. Luke describes Jesus as 'the Lord' eighteen times, e.g. 'when the Lord saw her he had compassion on her' (Luke 7.13). Matthew and Mark hardly ever call Jesus 'the Lord' and in John's Gospel the title is mainly used after the resurrection. But according to Luke the angel announced to the shepherds: 'To you is born this day in the city of David a Saviour who is Christ the Lord' (Luke 2.11).

In Luke's story of Jesus telling Simon Peter to let down his nets, when Peter caught the huge catch of fish he fell at Jesus's feet saying, 'Depart from me, for I am a sinful man, O Lord' (Luke 5.8). In this story Peter's response is like Isaiah's response when he saw God in the Temple (Isa. 6.5). A Christian who was reading the Old Testament could understand the title 'Lord' to mean that Jesus was divine. A pagan might have understood the story in a similar way.

MESSIAH, SERVANT, SON OF GOD

Like the other Gospel writers, Luke recognized Jesus as the Messiah, and he knew that Jesus had avoided calling Himself the Messiah during His lifetime. In the birth stories Luke presents Jesus as the Messiah, as the Son of God, and as the Suffering Servant:

The angel announces to Mary:

'He will be great, and will be called the Son of the Most High;
and the Lord God will give to him the throne of his father David,
and he will reign over the house of Jacob for ever;
and of his kingdom there will be no end.
... the child to be born will be called holy, the Son of God.' (Luke
1.32–33,35)

Simon, the devout old man, was 'looking for the consolation of
Israel, and the Holy Spirit was upon him. And it had been revealed to
him by the Holy Spirit that he should not see death before he had seen
the Lord's Christ' (Luke 2.25–26). When he took the child in his arms
he said:

'For my eyes have seen thy salvation
which thou hast prepared in the presence of all peoples,
a light for revelation to the Gentiles,
and for glory to thy people Israel' (Luke 2.30–32).

Luke also recalled the prophecies in Isaiah 40–66 about a servant of
the Lord who would take salvation to the nations of the world, and
who would suffer and would die (see Vol. 1, pp. 53, 55). Luke too saw
the Messiah as the Suffering Servant, and his Gospel contains a number
of references to the servant prophecies of Isaiah. He also records that
Jesus Himself, after the resurrection, explained that the Messiah had to
suffer: ' "Was it not necessary that the Christ should suffer these things
and enter into his glory?" And beginning with Moses and all the
prophets, he interpreted to them in all the scriptures the things
concerning himself' (Luke 24.26–27).

Luke shows that even as a boy Jesus was aware of God as His Father
(Luke 2.49). In his account of Jesus' ministry Luke records more
occasions when Jesus prayed than any other evangelist.

THE DEMANDS OF JESUS

Luke shows Jesus as the Lord who makes great demands on the people
who follow Him, as the Lord who is full of compassion, but at the same
time demands complete loyalty from His disciples. Luke records the
saying of Jesus that 'no one who puts his hand to the plough and looks
back is fit for the kingdom of God' (Luke 9.62). Luke also includes the
parables of counting the cost before building a tower, and before going
to war, and he concludes those parables with Jesus' words, 'Whoever
of you does not renounce all that he has cannot be my disciple' (Luke
14.33).

MATERIAL FOUND ONLY IN LUKE

The following is a brief outline of the material which appears only in
Luke's Gospel.

NARRATIVE

The birth of John the Baptist (Luke 1.5–80).
The angel appearing to Mary (Luke 1.26–38).
Mary and Joseph going to Bethlehem for the census (Luke 2.1–7).
The visit of the shepherds (Luke 2.8–20).
The circumcision of Jesus (Luke 2.21).
The presentation of Jesus in the Temple (Luke 2.22–40).
The boy Jesus going to Jerusalem for the Passover (Luke 2.41–52).
Jesus' family tree, back to Adam (Luke 3.23–38).
Jesus' sermon in Nazareth (Luke 4.16–20).
The widow's son at Nain (Luke 7.11–17).
The woman washing Jesus's feet with her tears (Luke 7.36–50).
The women disciples (Luke 8.1–3).
The unwelcoming Samaritans (Luke 9.51–56).
Martha and Mary's hospitality (Luke 10.38–41).
The woman blessing Jesus' mother (Luke 11.27–28).
The bent woman (Luke 13.10–17).
The Pharisees' warning about Herod (Luke 13.31–33).
The man with dropsy (Luke 14.1–6).
Ten lepers (Luke 17.11–19).
Zacchaeus (Luke 19.1–10).
Jesus' prayer for Simon Peter (Luke 22.31–33).
The angel and the drops of blood in Gethsemane (Luke 22.43–44).
Jesus' trial before Herod (Luke 23.6–12).
The weeping women following the cross (Luke 23.27–31).
The repentant robber (Luke 23.40–43).
The walk to Emmaus (Luke 24.13–35).

PARABLES

The two debtors (Luke 7.41–42).
The good Samaritan (Luke 10.25–42).
The friend at midnight (Luke 11.5–8).
The rich fool (Luke 12.13–21).
The fig tree (Luke 13.6–9).
The tower builder (Luke 14.28–30).
The king going to war (Luke 14.31–32).
The lost coin (Luke 15.8–10).
The prodigal son (Luke 15.11–32).
The dishonest steward (Luke 16.1–12).
The rich man and Lazarus (Luke 16.19–31).
A servant's duty (Luke 17.7–10).
The widow and the judge (Luke 18.1–8).
The Pharisee and the tax collector (Luke 18.9–14).

OTHER TEACHING

No one who puts his hand to the plough ... (Luke 9.62).
The need to be ready and waiting (Luke 12.35–38).
How to behave at feasts (Luke 14.7–14).
The days of Lot (Luke 17.28–30).

STUDY SUGGESTIONS

WORD STUDY

1. What is the meaning of the following words, as used in this chapter?
   (a) prologue   (b) continuous
2. What is meant by the statement that the details which Luke gives about times and dates help to 'authenticate' his account?

REVIEW OF CONTENT

3. Say in each case whether the following statements give a true or untrue account of the evidence in Luke's Gospel or elsewhere in the New Testament:
   (a) Luke was a doctor.
   (b) Paul calls Luke a Gentile.
   (c) Luke was a companion of Paul.
   (d) Luke witnessed the events of Jesus' life.
   (e) In his book Luke usually shows the Romans in a favourable light.
4. In what way are the birth stories in Luke different from those in Matthew?
5. Give examples of two ways in which Luke shows his interest in history.
6. To which of the following groups of people, according to Luke, did Jesus show a special sympathy and friendship? Give references to support your answers.
   (a) Herod and his supporters   (b) Pharisees and scribes
   (c) Sadducees (d) tax collectors (e) women (f) Samaritans
   (g) anyone who was despised by other people

BIBLE STUDY

7. Read Luke 1.24–56 and find the following details of 'time' which Luke had recorded:
   (a) For how long did Elizabeth hide her pregnancy?
   (b) In which month did the angel appear to Mary?
   (c) For how long did Mary stay with Elizabeth?
8. Read Luke 11.37–end. Which details in this passage show that:

(a) Jesus was the friend of Pharisees as well as tax collectors?
(b) Jesus knew the Old Testament well?
(c) Jesus was critical of some Jewish practices?
9. Luke writes about 'lawyers' (Luke 11.45f).
(a) What name do Matthew and Mark usually give to lawyers?
(b) For what particular reason do you think that Luke used the word 'lawyer'?

FURTHER STUDY AND DISCUSSION

10. Which groups of people are rejected and despised in your country today, and *why* are they rejected and despised? Do such people find they are welcome and accepted in your Church? Are there any such people in your own congregation?
11. 'Jesus' attitude to women was very different from that of other rabbis' (p. 52). What is the position of women: (a) in your community? (b) in your Church?
Is your Church faithful to the example of Jesus as portrayed by Luke?
12. 'He set his face to go to Jerusalem' Luke 9.51. How important do you think Jerusalem and Palestine are for the Church today? How far does Jerusalem's significance as a centre for Christians, Jews and Muslims help or hinder relationships between the three faiths?
13. How far do you think Luke's historical and geographical emphasis makes his Gospel specially helpful – or *un*helpful – in the Church's mission to the world today? Give your reasons.

THE ACTS OF THE APOSTLES

TRIUMPH OF THE GOSPEL

'A narrative of the things which have been accomplished among us' (Luke 1.1).

The first volume of Luke's book took the story of Jesus from His birth to His ascension, but 'the things which have been accomplished' did not end with Jesus' ascension. They continued in the life of the Church. The second volume, which we usually call simply 'Acts', is an account of the birth, life and work of the Church. We have already considered much of the story contained in Acts when we studied the growth of the Church (Vol. 1, ch. 5).

A THEOLOGICAL BOOK

The '*kerygma*' is the proclamation of the saving acts of God. In both volumes of his book Luke proclaims those saving acts. In the Gospel he proclaimed what God had done in Jesus, through an account of His life, death and resurrection. In Acts he proclaims that God is still at work, that the risen Jesus is alive and at work in His Church. As shown in the diagram below, Luke followed the same sort of pattern in Acts as he did in his Gospel.

Luke's Gospel	Acts
An angel promises the coming of Jesus	Jesus promises the Holy Spirit
The birth of Jesus	The birth of the Church through the coming of the Holy Spirit
Jesus' ministry of preaching, teaching and healing	The Church's ministry of preaching, teaching and healing
Jesus' obedience results in suffering	The Church's obedience results in suffering
God triumphs over suffering	God triumphs over suffering
The Scriptures have been fulfilled (e.g. Luke 24.25–27)	The Scriptures have been fulfilled (e.g. Acts 2.16–21)

Just as Jesus had preached to the crowds that gathered, so did the early Christians (e.g. Acts 3.11—4.4). Just as Jesus and His disciples had shared their money, so the first Christians shared their possessions (e.g. Acts 2.45; 4.34–37). Just as the resurrection of Jesus came through suffering and death, so through the sufferings and death of Christians growth and life came to the Church (e.g. Acts 11.19–26).

All through Acts Luke shows how the early Christians were guided by God, through the Holy Spirit. He describes how the Holy Spirit sends Christians to the people and the places that God has chosen for them (e.g. Acts 8.26,39–40; 16.6–10); God acts miraculously to release His people from prison (e.g. Acts 5.17–21; 12.6–11), and through God's clear guidance the Gentiles are admitted to the Church (e.g. Acts 10.1—11.18). Many people think that a better name for the Acts of the Apostles would be 'The Acts of the Holy Spirit'.

The 'acts' which Luke records are also the acts of the risen and ascended Jesus. This point is clearly made in the account of the healing of the lame man: 'The God of our fathers glorified his servant Jesus . . . And his name, by faith in his name, has made this man strong whom you see and know; and the faith which is through Jesus has given the man this perfect health in the presence of you all' (Acts 3.13–16).

This passage from one of Peter's speeches shows us the other way in which God's acts are proclaimed in the Acts of the Apostles. In the apostles' speeches as recorded by Luke we are constantly reminded of what God did in the life, death and resurrection of Jesus. For example, on the Day of Pentecost Peter spoke to a great crowd, and explained the gift of the Spirit: 'Men of Israel, hear these words: Jesus of Nazareth, a man attested to you by God with mighty works and wonders and signs which God did through him in your midst, as you yourselves know – this Jesus, delivered up according to the definite plan and foreknowledge of God, you crucified by the hands of lawless men . . . This Jesus God raised up, and of that we are all witnesses. Being therefore exalted at the right hand of God, and having received from the Father the promise of the Holy Spirit, he has poured out this which you see and hear' (Acts 2.22,32–33).

A HISTORICAL APPROACH

Although Acts is not simply a history book it is our main source of information about the early Church. Because the kerygma centred on God's actions in human history, the details of history were an important part of the proclamation. Luke records the names of many Roman officials, such as Sergius Paulus, Gallio, Felix and Festus (Acts 13.7; 18.12; 23.26; 24,27). Acts is also full of details of time and place, e.g. 'we sailed away from Philippi after the days of Unleavened Bread, and in five days we came to them at Troas, where we stayed for seven days' (Acts 20.6).

Some scholars have doubted whether Luke was always historically accurate. In Acts 5.36–37, for example, Gamaliel refers to two men who led unsuccessful rebellions against the Romans, Theudas and later Judas the Galilean. The Jewish historian Josephus, on the other hand, wrote about a rebel called Theudas who not only lived *after* Judas the Galilean, but was active after Gamaliel was speaking. However, Theudas was a common name, and there may have been more than one rebel leader with that name.

A more serious problem arises when we try to reconcile Luke's account with the details which we find in some of Paul's letters, as in Galatians 1.11—2.10, where Paul describes his own conversion and his relationship with the Church in Jerusalem. The details which Paul gives in Galatians do not wholly confirm the details which Luke gives us in Acts. For example, Luke says that Paul spoke boldly in Jerusalem, disputing with the Hellenists (Acts 9.28–29), while Paul himself states that he was not known by sight to the Churches of Judaea (Gal. 1.22). Possibly Paul meant the Judaean Churches outside Jerusalem. We must also remember that Paul and Luke were not writing the same kind of book, and had different purposes in writing. Paul was emphasizing to the Galatians that his missionary activity was not dependent on the Jerusalem Church. Luke was writing a more general description of events which he had not witnessed, and illustrating a geographical theme which we shall consider below. Luke may not have been correct in every single historical detail, but that is no reason to doubt his general historical accuracy, e.g. an inscription found in Delphi in central Greece shows us that there was a Gallio who became proconsul of Achaia, probably in July, AD 51 (Acts 18.12).

A GEOGRAPHICAL APPROACH

Luke has a geographical approach to the story of the Church, as he does to the ministry of Jesus. He begins Acts with an account of Jesus giving the disciples His final promise, that they would witness to Him 'in Jerusalem and in all Judaea and Samaria and to the end of the earth' (Acts 1.8). In the rest of the book Luke shows how this promise was fulfilled, beginning with the birth of the Church in Jerusalem and ending with Paul in Rome proclaiming the gospel to everyone who came to him.

A SELECTIVE ACCOUNT

Luke could not possibly have written down every event in the life of the early Church. When writing the Gospels he and the other writers had to select which stories they would tell about Jesus, and which they would leave out. Luke had to be even more selective when he was writing an account of the Church. Acts has a list of the names of the twelve apostles (Acts 1.13), but Peter, James and John are the only ones about whom Luke tells us any more. He writes about the appointment of the Seven (Acts 6.1–6), but five of them he does not mention again.

SECOND-HAND INFORMATION

Luke was not present when the disciples were filled with the Spirit at Pentecost. He did not witness the early events in Jerusalem. In order to write about those events he had to collect information from other people in the same way that he had collected stories about Jesus. Probably when he visited Jerusalem, and as he travelled round Palestine, he asked the Christians in each place about the things that had happened there (Acts 21.15,17).

FIRST-HAND INFORMATION

A number of passages in Acts are written in the first person plural: 'As

'For Luke the spread of the message and the growth of the Church showed the triumph of the Gospel,' a growth and a spread that still continue. In the Philippines, where Spanish colonists carried the message four centuries ago, 90 per cent of the people are Christian, and Church festivals are marked by colourful processions. In South India the Church is still a tiny minority, but people like this student and his wife can study the New Testament in their own languages, and read the stories of Jesus to their children.

61

we were going to the place of prayer' (Acts 16.16). Paul describes Luke as a companion, and Luke probably travelled with Paul on some of his journeys. Possibly he first joined Paul in Troas, on Paul's second journey. At that point in Luke's narrative he suddenly starts using 'we' where previously he has used 'they': 'When he' [i.e. Paul] 'had seen the vision, immediately we sought to go on into Macedonia' (Acts 16.10). Scholars consider that it is reasonable to suppose that when Luke wrote 'we' he was writing about events which he had witnessed and shared in.

Luke did not write about himself. He may have been converted through Paul's preaching, but we do not know. All that we know about Luke is what we deduce from his books, and what we read in Paul's letters (see p. 46). We may easily understand that Luke probably preferred to write about the events and people that he knew best. For this reason the greater part of his story of the Church is also the story of Paul.

THE TRIUMPH OF THE GOSPEL

Luke's association with Paul seems to have shaped his account of the Church. He showed the gospel being preached from Jerusalem to Rome through the missionary activity of Paul, but we know that the gospel had been preached in Rome long before Paul got there. Paul had written a letter to the Christians in Rome, and Luke tells how they were welcomed by the Christians there: 'And so we came to Rome. And the brethren there, when they heard of us, came as far as the Forum of Appius and the Three Taverns to meet us. On seeing them Paul thanked God and took courage' (Acts 28.15).

Although Luke wrote about Peter, James and John, he does not give us much information. Christian tradition has always been that Peter founded the Church in Rome. Paul's letters show that Peter had visited Antioch and suggests that he may have had connections with Corinth (Gal. 2.11; 1 Cor. 1.12), but Luke, who was writing from his personal point of view, had no reason to mention those facts.

However, Luke is far more than a biographer of Paul. There are distinctive features in Luke's theology which we do not find in the writings of Paul. For example, Luke seems to assume that speaking in tongues is proof of the gift of the Spirit (see Vol. 1, ch. 5). For Luke the spread of the gospel message to the ends of the earth and the growth of the Church show the triumph of the gospel.

STUDY SUGGESTIONS

WORDS AND MEANINGS

1. What is meant by the statement that Luke was 'selective' in his story of the Church?

2. In what way could you describe 'things which have been accomplished'?
3. What did Luke mean by 'the days of Unleavened Bread' (Acts 20.6)?
4. What do the words 'companion' and 'fellow-worker' mean to you?

REVIEW OF CONTENT

5. Why is it incorrect to think of Acts as only a history book?
6. Describe two ways in which Luke proclaims God's saving acts in the Acts of the Apostles.
7. Explain why such a large part of Acts is about Paul.
8. (a) Give one detail recorded by Luke in Acts which may not be totally accurate.
   (b) Give one detail recorded in Acts which can be dated by evidence outside the New Testament.
9. Who was Josephus?
10. What is the 'geographical' theme of Acts?
11. What can we deduce from the passages in Acts which Luke wrote in the first person plural (using 'we' instead of 'they').
12. What did Luke take to be proof of:
    (a) the gift of the Spirit?
    (b) the triumph of the gospel?

BIBLE STUDY

13. (a) What was the name of the tribune who saved Paul from a Jewish plot to kill him, according to Acts 23.12–30?
    (b) Using the references given on p. 59, find out what positions were held by: (a) Sergius Paulus (b) Felix (c) Porcius Festus
14. Read Acts 28.7–17. How many details can you find in this passage: (a) about *time*? (b) about *places*?
15. Read the account of Paul's first missionary journey in Acts 13.1 – 14.28. Which group of people, according to Luke, most often stirred up trouble for Paul?
16. Read Galatians 2.11–14. Use the cross-reference system in your Bible to see if the events recorded here are also recorded in Acts. How does this story add to our knowledge of the early Church?

FURTHER STUDY AND DISCUSSION

17. Do people in your Church speak in tongues? Do you know of other Churches where people speak in tongues? Would you agree with Luke's view that speaking in tongues is evidence of the gift of the Holy Spirit? Give reasons for your answer.
18. In this century the gospel has indeed spread 'to the ends of the

earth'. How far does this mean that the gospel has triumphed? Give examples to support your answer.

19. According to Luke's account of the Church in Acts, the Holy Spirit led the early Christians to overcome the barrier which divided Jews from Gentiles. What barriers divide your own society? Which of these barriers have already been overcome in the Church? Which ones remain, and how can they be overcome?

20. Luke wrote Acts to proclaim what God had done in the Church. What can you say God has done in the life of your own Church?— in your own personal life?

5
The Gospel According to John

The viewpoint of the writer of the Fourth Gospel, in telling the story of Jesus, is different from that of the other evangelists. Much of the information in John's Gospel is similar to the stories in the Synoptic Gospels: Jesus performs miracles; He mixes with all kinds of people, from learned Pharisees to Samaritan women; He comes into conflict with the Jewish leaders; He is betrayed by Judas Iscariot, accused before Pilate, crucified, and He rises on the third day. Yet there is also much material which appears *only* in this Gospel. Many of the Synoptic stories are omitted, and even the Synoptic stories that are included are told in a different style.

New Testament scholars do not agree about the relationship between John's Gospel and the Synoptic Gospels. Some think the writer knew and used Mark or Luke. Others think that this account is completely independent of the Synoptics.

There has been a great deal of discussion about who wrote this Gospel. Many books have been written on the subject, and many theories put forward. Here we shall leave the question of authorship until after we have had a look at the Gospel itself. In the meantime we shall simply refer to the author as 'John'.

FOUR GOSPELS

We shall be considering what is distinctive, and therefore what is different, about John's Gospel. However we should not forget that the Fourth Gospel was written for the same purpose as the others, i.e. to proclaim Jesus as 'the Christ'; 'these (things) are written that you may believe that Jesus is the Christ, the Son of God, and that believing you may have life in his name' (John 20.31).

Having four Gospels means that we are able to see Jesus from four different points of view. This gives us a much fuller picture of Him than we could get from reading a single Gospel. We can illustrate this very simply. Suppose your friend has gone to live in another town and he sends you a photograph of the house where he is living. If he sends a single photograph it will give you some idea of the building. If he sends you several photographs, one taken from the north, one taken from the south, and some taken of the interior of the house, you will have a much more complete picture. Each of the four Gospels is a profound theological book, with each evangelist proclaiming Jesus from his own viewpoint, as he saw and understood Him. No one ever understands another person fully and completely, so we should not expect that any of the Gospel writers had a complete understanding of Jesus. The differences between the four Gospels need not be seen as 'problems'. Instead they can enrich our understanding and add to our picture of Jesus.

THE GOSPEL OF LOVE

THE BEGINNING OF THE GOSPEL

'In the beginning was the Word,
and the Word was with God,
and the Word was God . . .
all things were made through him,
and without him was not anything made that
was made . . .
And the Word became flesh
and dwelt among us, full of grace and truth;
we have beheld his glory,
glory as of the only Son from the Father.'
(John 1.1,14)

Mark began his account of Jesus with the story of John the Baptist, and Proto-Luke may have begun in the same way. Luke and Matthew began with an account of the birth of Jesus. Matthew traced Jesus' ancestry back to Abraham, and Luke traced it back to Adam. John goes a step further, and states that the Word of God which existed before the beginning of time became flesh in Jesus. The hymn which introduces John's Gospel, sometimes called the Prologue, is a summary of the writer's belief about who Jesus is and what He has done.

THE TIME OF JESUS'S MINISTRY

According to John the ministry of Jesus and the ministry of John the Baptist overlapped for a time: 'After this Jesus and his disciples went into the land of Judaea; there he remained with them and baptized. John also was baptizing . . . For John had not yet been put in prison' (John 3.22–24). These verses also mention a ministry in Judaea before Jesus' ministry in Galilee, although there is no hint of such a ministry in the Synoptics. Matthew and Mark simply record that Jesus began His ministry in Galilee after John the Baptist was arrested (Matt. 4.12; Mark 1.14).

None of the Gospel writers actually states how long Jesus' ministry lasted. Luke records that Jesus was about thirty years old when He began (Luke 3.23), but like the other Synoptic writers he only records a single Passover during the period of the ministry. This might mean that Jesus' ministry lasted for less than one year. However, John records in

66

three passages that it was Passover time: 'The Passover of the Jews was at hand' (John 2.13; cf. 6.4; 13.1). This seems to suggest that Jesus' ministry lasted for between two and three years.

In two passages John's details concerning the timing of events are noticeably different from the Synoptic accounts. John places the cleansing of the Temple at the beginning of Jesus' ministry instead of at the end (John 2.13–22). He also places the crucifixion a day earlier than in the Synoptics. In John's account Jesus died at the same time as the Passover lambs were being killed in the Temple courtyard, so although John records that Jesus ate a final supper with His disciples, it would not have been the Passover meal. According to John, Jesus was dead by the time that meal was being eaten (Matt. 26.17ff; Mark 14.12ff; Luke 22.7ff; John 19.14).

THE PLACE OF JESUS' MINISTRY

FOCUS ON JERUSALEM

None of the Synoptic writers mentions any visit of Jesus to Jerusalem during His ministry until the final week of His life. John records at least three earlier visits (John 2.13; 5.1; 7.10; 10.22), and describes two miracles that took place during those visits (John 5.2–9; 9.1–7). He records Jesus doing a great deal of teaching in Jerusalem and in the Temple.

Probably John was correct in this matter. Palestine was only a small country, and every Jew thought of Jerusalem as his spiritual home. Whenever it was possible Jewish men went to Jerusalem for the three great festivals. We have noticed that Luke records Jesus staying in Bethany, and that He was probably visiting Jerusalem at the time (p. 50). Both Matthew and Luke record Jesus' lament over Jerusalem: 'O Jerusalem, Jerusalem, killing the prophets and stoning those who are sent to you! How often would I have gathered your children together as a hen gathers her brood under her wings, but you would not! Behold, your house is forsaken and desolate. For I tell you, you will not see me again, until you say, "Blessed is he who comes in the name of the Lord"' (Matt. 23.37–39; cf. Luke 13.34–35). Clearly these words were spoken by someone who knew and loved Jerusalem. Yet if we read only Matthew's Gospel we would think they were spoken by Jesus on His first visit to Jerusalem. Luke records a visit by Jesus when He was twelve but does not record any later ones, and he tells of Jesus speaking these words long before He had reached the city.

NAMES AND DESCRIPTIONS OF PLACES

One of the characteristics of John's Gospel is its great number of references to place-names and exact locations. 'Now there is in Jerusalem by the Sheep Gate a pool, in Hebrew called Bethzatha, which has five porticoes' (John 5.2). The places where Jesus healed people and where He taught are often described in detail: 'It was the feast of the dedication at Jerusalem; it was winter, and Jesus was walking in the Temple, in the portico of Solomon' (John 10.22). Solomon's portico is known to us (see Vol. 1, p. 11) from the writing of Josephus. In this century archaeological discoveries have shown how accurate some of John's descriptions are. Archaeologists have discovered the remains of a pool with five porticoes (cf. John 5.2). They have also found a great paved courtyard which could be the 'place called The Pavement, and in Hebrew, Gabbatha', where Pilate brought Jesus out and sat on the judgement seat (John 19.13).

JESUS' MIRACLES

SEVEN MIRACLES

Like all the Gospel writers John had to be selective. He knew that Jesus had worked many miracles: 'Now Jesus did many other signs in the presence of the disciples which are not written in this book . . .' (John 20.30), but he only described a few, traditionally counted as seven:
The wedding feast at Cana (John 2.1–11).
Healing the official's son (John 4.46–53).
The cripple by the Pool of Bethzatha (John 5.1–9).
Feeding the five thousand (John 6.1–14).
Jesus walking on the water (John 6.16–21).
Healing the blind man (John 9.1–7).
The raising of Lazarus (John 11.1–44).
Of these seven miracles, three have parallels in the other Gospels. The feeding of the five thousand and the walking on the water are clearly the same events as those described in the Synoptics. Probably the account of healing the official's son is another version of the 'Q' story about the centurion's servant (Matt. 8.5–10; Luke 7.1–10). Matthew wrote that the centurion's 'boy' was sick. 'Boy' could mean a son or a servant. Luke took it to mean a servant. In John's account the centurion is just 'an official', and it is his son who is sick. The remaining four miracles are peculiar to John. It is surprising to find that John has recorded no stories about Jesus casting out demons.

MIRACLES AS SIGNS

John selected the miracles which he felt pointed most clearly to Jesus as the Christ: 'these are written that you may believe that Jesus is the Christ, the Son of God' (John 20.31). For John, the miracles were 'signs'. They pointed to the truth about who Jesus was, and they pointed ahead to His death on the cross.

The writers of the Synoptic Gospels also believed that the miracles were signs. For that reason Matthew collected together nine miracles which pointed to the Messiahship of Jesus. However, the Synoptic writers do not bring out the meaning of Jesus' miracles in the same way that John does. In John's account of the feeding of the five thousand he describes the event itself in fifteen verses, and then takes thirty-five verses to record Jesus' teaching that He Himself is the bread of life (John 6.1–15; 25–60). In several instances a whole chapter of John's Gospel is given to describing a miracle and explaining its meaning. In John 9.1–41 we have an account of Jesus healing a man born blind and teaching that He is the light of the world. In John 11.1–44 Jesus claims to be 'the resurrection and the life', and shows the truth of His claim by raising Lazarus who had been dead for four days.

JESUS' TEACHING IN JOHN

THE FORM

In John's Gospel Jesus' teaching is given in what is called a 'discursive' form. The characteristic pattern is that Jesus makes a statement, e.g. 'Do not labour for the food which perishes, but for the food which endures to eternal life' (John 6.27), and is led on by His hearers' questions to 'discourse', or speak more fully on the subject, and explain more clearly what He means.

Most of the teaching which is recorded in John's Gospel was apparently given to individuals, e.g. Nicodemus, Martha (John 3.1ff.; 11.20–27), or to small groups of people, either Jewish officials or His disciples. What we have in this Gospel is an account of Jesus speaking in discussion rather than preaching to great crowds of people.

PICTURE LANGUAGE

(a) *Parables*: There are no story parables in John to compare with the parables of the sower or the good Samaritan. However, John includes a number of short parables:
The wind (John 3.8).
The bridegroom and his friend (John 3.29).
The apprentice son (John 5.19–20a).
The slave and the son (John 8.35).
The shepherd, the thief and the doorkeeper (John 10.1–5).
The traveller at night (John 11.9–10).
The grain of wheat (John 12.24).
The pains of childbirth (John 16.21).
(b) *'I am' Sayings*: The famous 'I am' sayings of Jesus are all found in John's Gospel:
I am the bread of life (John 6.35).

I am the light of the world (John 9.5).
I am the door of the sheep (John 10.7).
I am the good shepherd (John 10.11).
I am the resurrection and the life (John 11.25).
I am the way, the truth and the life (John 14.6).
I am the true vine (John 15.1).

THE MEANING OF THE TEACHING

Many scholars believe that what we have in John's Gospel is not so much the actual words that Jesus spoke, but more the writer's understanding of what His words meant. There is little doubt, however, that John has recorded many genuine sayings of Jesus. Some of them have been recorded in almost identical words by the Synoptic writers, for example:

'He who loves his life loses it, and he who hates his life in this world will keep it for eternal life' (John 12.25)	'For whoever would save his life will lose it; and whoever loses his life for my sake, he will save it' (Luke 9.24).
'He who receives anyone whom I send receives me; and he who receives me receives him who sent me' (John 13.20).	'He who receives you receives me, and he who receives me receives him who sent me' (Matt. 10.40).

In some parts of John's Gospel, however, we cannot tell where Jesus' words end and the writer's interpretation of them begins. In English and many other languages, spoken words are shown by printing quotation marks ('...' or "...") before and after them. But this is not the case in John's original Greek. The passage beginning 'God so loved the world ...' in John 3.16–21, for example, might seem to be a continuation of what Jesus was saying to Nicodemus in vv. 15–20. But in many Bibles it has no quotation marks. The Greek text does not make it clear whether the writer was continuing to quote words spoken by Jesus, or giving his own interpretation of the preceding verses. Perhaps it is not important for us to know. The evangelist had thought deeply about Jesus' words, and wanted to record not only the teaching itself but also his own understanding of it.

JOHN'S UNDERSTANDING OF JESUS AND HIS DISCIPLES

JESUS THE MAN

Like the other evangelists, John wanted to show that Jesus was a real human being. Therefore he included details about Jesus being hungry, tired and thirsty: 'Jesus, wearied as he was with his journey, sat down beside the well', and then He asked the woman who came to the well to give Him a drink. When the disciples returned from the town with the food they had bought, they 'besought him, saying "Rabbi, eat"' (John 4.6–7, 31).

John's story of the raising of Lazarus shows Jesus as a man who felt deep emotion. 'Then Mary ... fell at his feet, saying to him, "Lord, if you had been here, my brother would not have died." When Jesus saw her weeping, and the Jews who came with her also weeping, he was deeply moved in spirit and troubled; and he said, "Where have you laid him?" They said to him, "Lord, come and see." Jesus wept. So the Jews said, "See how he loved him!" ... Then Jesus, deeply moved again, came to the tomb.' (John 11.32–38.)

In this Gospel, Jesus' disciples usually call Him 'Rabbi' ('my master', see Vol. 1, p. 30) or 'Lord' (or 'Sir', see p. 53). 'You call me Teacher and Lord; and you are right, for so I am' (John 13.13). However, John never allows his readers to forget that Jesus is more than an ordinary man. When the disciples beg Him to eat He tells them, 'I have food to eat of which you do not know ... My food is to do the will of him who sent me, and to accomplish his work' (John 4.32–34).

JESUS THE SON

John placed great emphasis on the special relationship which Jesus had with God. In John, Jesus sometimes refers to Himself as 'Son of man', but more often calls Himself simply 'the Son': 'If the Son makes you free, you will be free indeed' (John 8.36). Occasionally He speaks of 'the Son of God': 'This illness is not unto death; it is for the glory of God, so that the Son of God may be glorified by means of it' (John 11.4).

Even more important than Jesus' name for Himself is His name for God. In John's Gospel Jesus uses the word 'Father' more than 100 times. He says 'the Father', 'my Father', and in prayer simply 'Father'. John does not record Jesus going away into the hills to be alone and pray, but he does record a very long prayer of Jesus on the last night of His life (John 17.1–26).

Throughout the Gospel John makes it clear that Jesus' authority results from His close relationship with the Father, which is one of love: 'The Father loves the Son', 'I love the Father' (John 3.35; 14.31). Jesus calls His disciples His friends because they respond to His love for them by loving and obeying Him and by loving each other (see John 13.34–35). Jesus' friends are included in the special relationship of love and unity which the Son has with His Father: 'He who loves me will be loved by my Father, and I will love him' (see John 14.20–23).

John shows Jesus always being fully in control of events. He changed water into wine in order to reveal His glory, not because His Mother asked Him (John 2.4,11). No one could arrest Him until 'the hour had

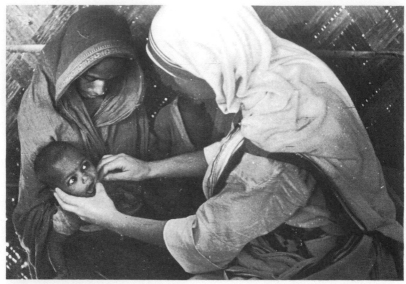

The Fourth Gospel has been called the Gospel of Love. 'John makes it clear that Jesus called His disciples His friends because they responded to His love by loving and obeying Him, and by loving each other.' Many Christians today would probably think of Mother Teresa as the most perfect example of Christian love in action, spending her life in selfless service of the sick and poor in Calcutta.

And for some Christians loving and obeying God means not only spending but *losing* their lives, in order to proclaim Jesus as the Christ – like William Tyndale who was burnt as a heretic for putting the Bible into English so that people could read it for themselves (see p. 119).

come', and even then the soldiers were not able to seize Him; He gave Himself up to them (John 7.30; 19.11).

THE DISCIPLES

From John's Gospel we gain a lot of extra information about the disciples. In the Synoptic Gospels only Peter, James and John are shown as individuals. In John's Gospel Peter has an important position, but so do other members of the Twelve. Andrew, who is only mentioned as Simon Peter's brother in the Synoptic tradition, appears in John as a man who introduces others to Jesus. Andrew introduces Peter, the boy with the loaves and fishes, and a group of Greeks (John 1.40–42; 6.8; 12.22). Philip and Thomas also appear as individuals in this Gospel. Surprisingly, James and John are mentioned only once, and are called simply 'the sons of Zebedee' (John 21.2).

There are six passages in John's Gospel where the writer speaks of a disciple whom he does not name. On four occasions he describes the disciple as one 'whom Jesus loved' (John 13.23; 19.26; 21.7,20). We shall consider the identity of the so-called 'Beloved Disciple' later, for he is closely connected with the writing of this Gospel.

A GOSPEL WRITTEN WITH HINDSIGHT

More than any other of the Gospels this Gospel has been written with hindsight. The writer was not so much interested in showing Jesus as people knew Him during His ministry. He knew that during Jesus' lifetime the disciples did not understand who He was or what He was doing. He records that Jesus once said to them 'What I am doing you do not know now, but afterward you will understand' (John 13.7). In two passages he states that at the time the disciples did not understand, but after the resurrection they remembered and understood (John 2.22; 12.16). The author's purpose in writing this Gospel was to show Jesus as he had come to understand Him.

STUDY SUGGESTIONS

WORDS AND MEANINGS

1. Explain the meaning of the following words as used in this chapter:
   (a) location   (b) discursive   (c) identity
2. What is meant by the statement that John's Gospel was written with 'hindsight'?

REVIEW OF CONTENT

3. What do we gain from having *four* Gospels?
4. How far back does John trace the origins of Jesus?

5. Name two places in Jerusalem which are described by John, and which have been discovered by archaeologists?
6. Name two disciples who are only listed as names in the Synoptic Gospels, but also appear several times in John's Gospel.
7. (a) Why does the writer of the Fourth Gospel call the miracles of Jesus 'signs'?
   (b) In what other ways does he emphasize the significance of the miracles?
8. Describe two of the ways in which Jesus' teaching is presented differently in John's Gospel from the Synoptics.
9. In what chief way does John emphasize Jesus' special relationship with God?

BIBLE STUDY

10. Use the cross-reference system in your Bible to discover which other book in the Bible starts with the words 'In the beginning'.
    (b) Why do you think that John started his Gospel with those same words?
11. Find the following stories in John's Gospel, and then use the cross-reference system in your Bible to discover whether they appear in any other Gospel. Give the references for any that do appear.
    (a) Changing water into wine at Cana (John 2.1–11).
    (b) Nicodemus comes to Jesus by night (John 3.1–21).
    (c) The Samaritan woman by the well (John 4.7–26).
    (d) The crown of thorns and the purple robe (John 19.1–3).
    (e) The spear thrust in Jesus' side (John 19.34).
    (f) Joseph of Arimathea and Nicodemus took Jesus' body and put it in the tomb (John 19.38–39).
12. Use a concordance or the cross-reference system to discover whether the following stories recorded in the Synoptic Gospels can also be found in John. Give the references for any that can.
    (a) The Transfiguration (Matt. 17.1–8)
    (b) Jairus's daughter (Matt. 9.18–26)
    (c) Jesus' triumphant entry into Jerusalem (Matt. 21.1–11)
    (d) The widow's penny (Mark 12.41–44)
    (e) Three hours of darkness and the curtain of the Temple torn in two (Matt. 27.45,51)

FURTHER STUDY AND DISCUSSION

13. John 3.16 is one of the best-known verses in the New Testament. Is it important to know whether Jesus Himself actually spoke those words? Give reasons for your answer.
14. Often our view of what a person is like changes after knowing that person for a long time. Which is most likely to be correct, our early

opinion or our later one? What does your answer suggest to you about the four evangelists' views of Jesus?

15. Thomas is known for being the disciple who doubted the truth of the Resurrection (John 20.24–29). What value do you consider that doubt has:
(a) in the lives of individual Christians?
(b) in the life of the Church?

16. 'Jesus' authority results from His close relationship with the Father, (p. 71). Read John 7.14–18 and 10.37–38, and then say what gives the Church and individual Christians today authority to preach and teach in the name of Jesus.

AUTHORSHIP: LINKS WITH THE 'BELOVED DISCIPLE'?

'This is the disciple who is bearing witness to these things, and who has written these things; and we know that his testimony is true' (John 21.24).

EDITOR'S NOTES

These words at the end of John's Gospel have been written by someone who was not the author, whom we call an 'editor'. We cannot be certain whether the editor added just the last two verses (John 21.24–25), or whether he added the whole of John 21. Many scholars think that the whole chapter was added by an editor. The last two verses of chapter 20 (John 20.30–31) sound as if they are the conclusion of the Gospel. If the writer himself had added another chapter he would probably have moved his concluding words to the end of it.

There is no evidence to show who the editor was. The words 'We know' in v. 24 suggest that the person who wrote this verse was giving the views of a group of people. Perhaps he belonged to a group which had followed one of the disciples and been influenced by his views. Biblical scholars refer to a 'Johannine school' of thought and tradition. This takes account of the fact that the Letters of John and the Gospel of John contain many of the same ideas and expressions, although they may have been written by different people. To call a particular way of thinking 'Johannine' does not necessarily mean that it began with the disciple John. It means that it is a way of looking at things which is characteristic of the Gospel and the Letters of John.

The editor identifies the disciple about whom he is writing as the Beloved Disciple (see John 21.20–23).

THE BELOVED DISCIPLE

The editor claims that the Beloved Disciple had witnessed the events of Jesus' life, death and resurrection. He had either written them down himself, or caused them to be written down. If we could be certain who the Beloved Disciple was, we might be closer to knowing who wrote the Fourth Gospel.

The Beloved Disciple appears in four passages in John's Gospel. (1) He was present at the last supper: 'One of the disciples, whom Jesus loved, was lying close to the breast of Jesus' (John 13.23ff). (2) He witnessed the Crucifixion and Jesus gave His mother into his care (John 19.26–27). (3) He was with Peter when Mary Magdalene brought the news of the empty tomb. He outran Peter but let Peter enter the tomb first, 'then . . . also went in, and he saw and believed' (John 20.2–10). (4) The Beloved Disciple was present when Jesus appeared to the disciples by the Sea of Tiberias. He was the first to recognize that the stranger on the beach was Jesus (John 21.1–23).

It seems as if the Beloved Disciple had just died when the final editorial comment was written. Apparently there had been a popular belief that Jesus had promised to return before that disciple died. The editor carefully points out that Jesus had not made any such promise; He had simply said to Peter that His will for the Beloved Disciple was none of Peter's business: 'The saying spread abroad among the brethren that this disciple was not to die; yet Jesus did not say to him that he was not to die, but, "If it is my will that he remains until I come, what is that to you?" ' (John 21.23).

There have been many theories about the identity of the Beloved Disciple. The following are a few of them:

1. *John the son of Zebedee*. This was the traditional belief of the ancient Church. In the Synoptic Gospels Peter, James and John appear as the three disciples who were closest to Jesus (see Vol. 1, p. 35), and who on some occasions were the only ones to be with Him. John is mentioned three times in Acts, always in close association with Peter. When Peter and John appeared before the Sanhedrin 'they perceived that they were uneducated common men' (Acts 4.13). According to Acts they were involved in the mission to Samaria (Acts 8.14–25). From Paul's letter to the Galatians we learn that Peter, John and James (the brother of Jesus, see Vol. 1, p. 109) became the leaders of the Church in Jerusalem, 'reputed to be pillars' (Gal. 2.9).

2. *Lazarus*. This theory is based on the fact that Lazarus is described in John's Gospel as 'he whom you love' (John 11.3).

3. *The Rich Young Ruler* who appears in the Synoptics, and of whom Mark writes 'Jesus looking upon him loved him' (Mark 10.21).

4. *Nicodemus*, who is only mentioned in connection with Jerusalem,

and who is described in this Gospel as being a secret disciple (John 19.38).

5. *An idealized person* who represents the true disciple of Christ, but who cannot be identified with any one of Jesus' disciples.

OTHER LEADERS CALLED JOHN

Five of the New Testament books are associated with the name of John: the Gospel, the three letters of John, and the Revelation (Vol. 1, chs. 7,8). 2 and 3 John were written by 'the elder', but he did not give his name. The writer of Revelation gave his name as John, but called himself a prophet.

Papias (see p. 23) clearly knew of two disciples called John: John the Apostle and John the Elder (or presbyter). He wrote, 'If anyone came who had been a follower of the elders, I inquired into the sayings of the elders – what Andrew said, or what Peter said, or what Philip, or Thomas, or James, or John, or Matthew, or any other of the disciples of the Lord said – and the things which Aristion and the Elder John, the disciples of the Lord, were saying' (see also p. 95).

Papias's statement is evidence of the existence of John the Elder, but it cannot be taken as evidence that John the Elder wrote either the Letters or the Gospel of John. Some people think that the Gospel, the Letters and the Revelation were written by three or more different people. But there is no way of knowing for certain who wrote any of these 'Johannine' writings, or the exact relationship between them.

THE EYE-WITNESS, THE
AUTHOR AND THE EDITORS OF THE GOSPEL

Even if we were able to identify the 'disciple who is bearing witness' we should still not be certain for how much of the Gospel he was responsible. 'These things' might refer just to the events described in chapter 21, or to the later chapters, or to the whole of the Gospel. The editor's further comment 'and who has written these things' can also be understood in various ways. It might mean that the Beloved Disciple had himself written a part or the whole of the Gospel. Or it might mean that someone else wrote the Gospel, using the record of what Jesus had done and the interpretation of His teaching received from the Beloved Disciple, as well as the results of his own study and meditation.

There is evidence in the Gospel to suggest that it has been edited in several places. One example is the Prologue. Jesus is not called 'the Word' anywhere else in the Gospel. Possibly the Prologue was added later because it summed up the whole of the Gospel. We cannot tell who wrote it, or who added it to the Gospel. It may have been the writer of the Gospel, or someone else. There are passages in John where the author appears to have a first-hand knowledge of Jerusalem and

Judaism. There are other passages where he appears to have very little knowledge of those things. This suggests that the writer (or editor) was using different sources of information.

There are many different theories about the relationship between the Beloved Disciple, the writer, and the editors of John's Gospel. Some scholars have thought that it was written very late, with a long chain of transmission from the Beloved Disciple to the final edition of the Gospel. Others have thought it was written early by the Beloved Disciple himself – who may or may not have been John the son of Zebedee. Every theory about this Gospel leaves some questions unanswered. But whatever the case may be, it seems to reflect on the one hand a specially close association with Jesus during His lifetime, and on the other a special concern for the deeper meaning of His death and resurrection, summed up in John 3.16–21. John's Gospel remains a profound and powerful witness to what has been described as 'the faith of the whole Bible, that God is love, and that there is no hope at all for the world without Him'

STUDY SUGGESTIONS

WORDS AND MEANINGS

1. Explain the difference between the work of a writer and the work of an editor.
2. What are 'concluding' words?
3. What word means 'belonging to John'?
4. What is the meaning of 'identify'?

REVIEW OF CONTENT

5. Which of the following statements can be made with any certainty:
   (a) The Beloved Disciple wrote the Fourth Gospel?
   (b) The Beloved Disciple witnessed the events of Jesus' life?
   (c) The editors of the Fourth Gospel claim that the witness of the Beloved Disciple is represented in the Gospel?
   (d) John the son of Zebedee was the Beloved Disciple?
   (e) There was a man called John the Elder?
   (f) John the Elder wrote the Fourth Gospel?

BIBLE STUDY

6. Read John 19.25–36. Is it possible to know who was the eye-witness mentioned in verse 35?
7. Read Acts 4.13 and John 7.14. Why do you suppose that both these verses are used in the arguments about whether John the Son of Zebedee wrote the Fourth Gospel?

FURTHER STUDY AND DISCUSSION

8. 'We beheld his glory' (John 1.14). In what way or ways have you yourself seen Christ's glory?
9. Is it important to know who wrote the Gospel according to John? Give reasons for your answer.
10. 'John's Gospel is theology, it is not history.' What do you think this statement means, and how far do you think it is true? Give your reasons.
11. 'The author's purpose was to show Jesus as he had come to understand Him.' (p. 73). In what special ways, if any, has your own study of John's Gospel helped to enrich your understanding of who Jesus was and what He was – and still is – doing?

6
The Old Testament in the New Testament

'They received the word with all eagerness, examining the scriptures daily to see if these things were so' (Acts 17.11).

The people who were examining the 'scriptures' were Jews in Beroea who had heard Paul and Barnabas preaching in the synagogue. The word 'scriptures' cannot refer to the Bible as we know it, for at that time the New Testament did not exist. When Paul was preaching in Beroea it is unlikely that any of the New Testament books had even been written. The Jews in Beroea were examining the *Jewish* Scriptures, the collection of sacred writings which we call the 'Old Testament'.

THE JEWISH SCRIPTURES

JEWISH SACRED WRITINGS

Many of the events in Jesus' life are said to have happened 'that the scripture might be fulfilled' (e.g. John 19.36). There are many other parts of the New Testament where we find the word 'scripture' being used. The literal meaning of 'scripture' is simply something that is 'written' (see Vol. 1, p. 1). For the Jews the word had come to mean the collection of books which they considered to be sacred. Specially trained scribes copied the words with great care, because they were holy words. They copied them on to leather scrolls which would last for a long time. The scrolls were kept in the synagogues. Old scrolls which had worn out were carefully collected together and kept in a special store-room in the synagogue called the *genizah*, and were finally buried with reverence. Even the leather itself had become holy.

The chief time when the Scriptures were read was during sabbath worship in the synagogue. Luke records that when Jesus was in the synagogue in Nazareth 'He stood up to read; and there was given to him the book of the prophet Isaiah. He opened the book and found the place' (Luke 4.17). Luke actually wrote that He 'unrolled the book', which shows that Jesus was reading from a scroll. It must be difficult to find the place in a long scroll. When Jesus had finished reading 'he rolled up the book and gave it back to the attendant' (Luke 4.20).

The Jews did not think of their Scriptures as a single book, or even as a single collection of books. There were three groups of books of varying importance. Most important of all was 'the Law'. Then came 'the Prophets'. Lastly there were 'the Writings'.

1. THE LAW

The Law, which the Jews called the *Torah*, was written on five scrolls, containing the first five books of our Old Testament: Genesis, Exodus, Leviticus, Numbers, Deuteronomy. We sometimes call them 'the Books of Moses' or 'the Pentateuch' (Greek, meaning 'five books'). The Jews thought of them as one book, not five. They called the Torah 'the Book of Moses': 'Have you not read in the Book of Moses?' (Mark 12.26).

The Law was the most important part of the Scriptures. The Sadducees believed that only the Law was truly from God. They did not accept the Prophets or the Writings as being Scripture. Jesus knew that, so He quoted from the Law when He was talking with Sadducees.

2. THE PROPHETS

The Prophets were divided into two groups.

(a) *The Former Prophets*: Joshua, Judges, Samuel and Kings. The Former Prophets were written on four scrolls. We think of them as history books, for they tell the story of Israel from the time they entered the Promised Land until they were taken away into captivity in Babylon. Like the Gospels they are really theological books, written with hindsight and interpreting events. For Jews the importance of the Former Prophets is that they tell what God has done. They show how God revealed Himself to Israel in the events of Israel's history and in the leaders that He sent them.

(b) *The Latter Prophets*: Isaiah, Jeremiah, Ezekiel and the Twelve. The Latter Prophets were also written on four scrolls. Isaiah, Jeremiah and Ezekiel were each long enough to fill a scroll. 'The Twelve' are Hosea, Joel, Amos, Obadiah, Jonah, Micah, Nahum, Habakkuk, Zephaniah, Haggai, Zechariah and Malachi. They are all short books, and at one time were all written on a single scroll. Christians often call Isaiah, Jeremiah and Ezekiel the 'Major Prophets', and the Twelve the 'Minor Prophets'. Major and Minor are Latin words meaning 'greater' and 'smaller', and refer to the length of the books, not to their importance.

3. THE WRITINGS

'The Writings' include all the other books of the Old Testament: Psalms, Proverbs, Job, Ezra-Nehemiah, Chronicles, Song of Solomon, Ruth, Lamentations, Ecclesiastes, Esther and Daniel. The most important book in this group was Psalms. According to Luke Jesus used the name 'Psalms' to mean the 'Writings': 'Then Jesus said to them, "These are my words which I spoke to you while I was with you, that everything written about me in the law of Moses and the prophets and the psalms must be fulfilled" ' (Luke 24.44).

At the time of Jesus the Jewish rabbis were not certain whether all the books in the Writings should be counted as Scripture. In particular they had doubts about the Song of Solomon and Esther. In about AD 100 a council of Pharisees in Jamnia finally agreed that they were Scripture.

OTHER NEW TESTAMENT WAYS OF REFERRING TO SCRIPTURE

1. 'IT IS WRITTEN'

When Jesus and the Devil were quoting Scripture at one another in the wilderness, it was enough for each of them to say 'It is written'.
'The devil . . . said to him, "if you are the Son of God, throw yourself down; for it is written,

'He will give his angels charge of you,' and
'On their hands they will bear you up,
lest you strike your foot against a stone.' "

Jesus said to him, "Again it is written, 'You shall not tempt the Lord your God' " ' (Matt. 4.5–7).
Paul often used the same expression in his letters (e.g. Gal. 3.10–13).

2. THE LAW

Jesus and the New Testament writers often refer to the law. 'They brought him up to Jerusalem to present him to the Lord (as it is written in the law of the Lord, "Every male that opens the womb shall be called holy to the Lord")' (Luke 2.23). The 'law' usually means the Torah, the Law of Moses.

3. THE PROPHETS

The New Testament is full of quotations from the Old Testament prophets: e.g. 'It is written in the prophets, "And they shall all be taught by God" ' (John 6.45). The early Christians were deeply impressed by the way in which the words of the prophets were fulfilled in Jesus. When they read a passage such as the following one from the prophet Isaiah, they found that they were reading a description of Jesus.

'Surely he has borne our griefs
and carried our sorrows;
yet we esteemed him stricken,
smitten by God and afflicted.

83

But he was wounded for our transgressions,
he was bruised for our iniquities;
upon him was the chastisement that made us whole,
and with his stripes we are healed . . .
And they made his grave with the wicked
and with a rich man in his death,
although he had done no violence,
and there was no deceit in his mouth.' (Isa. 53.4–5,9)

It was not only the writings of the prophets that seemed to point to Jesus; all the Jewish Scriptures seemed to speak of Him. Christians came to think of the whole Jewish Scriptures as prophecy. We find Matthew quoting from the book of Psalms and stating, 'this was to fulfil what was spoken by the prophet' (Matt. 13.34–35). For the evangelist the psalmist had become a prophet, because he had written about Jesus.

4. THE SACRED WRITINGS

In 2 Timothy we read, 'from childhood you have been acquainted with the sacred writings which are able to instruct you for salvation through faith in Christ Jesus. All scripture is inspired by God and profitable for teaching, for reproof, for correction and for training in righteousness' (2 Tim. 3.15–16). The writer of 2 Timothy cannot have meant the Bible, since the Bible as we know it did not exist at that time. 'The sacred writings' must mean the sacred writings of the Jews. The writer believed that the Old Testament could 'instruct for salvation' because it points to Jesus, and salvation comes through faith in Jesus. If he had meant the whole Bible, or even the New Testament, his message would have been the same. The Scriptures can instruct, but salvation is through Jesus.

There are only three books of the Old Testament which are not quoted by the New Testament writers. They are Ecclesiastes, Esther and the Song of Solomon.

THE LANGUAGE OF SCRIPTURE

The Old Testament was written in Hebrew, except for a very few chapters which were written in Aramaic (two words in Gen. 31.47; Ezra 4.8—6.18; 7.12–26; Jer. 10.11; Dan. 2.4b—7.28). Long before the time of Jesus the Jews had stopped using Hebrew as the ordinary language which they used every day. The Jews of Palestine and Babylon spoke Aramaic. Jews in Egypt and the West spoke Greek. In order to be able to understand their Scriptures the Jews needed translations.

TARGUMS, SEPTUAGINT, APOCRYPHA

Aramaic-speaking Jews had the *Targums*, which explained the text as well as translating it into Aramaic. Originally they were not written down, but later came to be so.

Greek-speaking Jews had the Septuagint, which was a written translation of the Old Testament in Greek. There was a legend that this translation had been made by seventy elders. For that reason it was called the Septuagint ('*Septuaginta*' is the Latin word for seventy). The Roman numeral for 70 is often used as an abbreviation for the Septuagint – LXX. The LXX is different in several respects from the Hebrew Old Testament. For example, in LXX the book of Job is only two-thirds the length of the Hebrew text. In Jeremiah and Ezekiel the chapters are in a different order. Some of the words have been given a different meaning.

Although the very first Christians were Palestinian Jews, it was not long before the majority of Christians were Greek-speaking. The Scripture that they used was therefore the Septuagint. There were more books in the Septuagint than in the Hebrew Scriptures, because the Palestinian rabbis rejected some of the books which Greek-speaking Jews accepted as Scripture. The Palestinian rabbis considered that some books had been written too recently to be Scripture, and other books had been written in Greek, not in Hebrew, and therefore could not be considered sacred. The books which were in the Septuagint but were not accepted by the rabbis in Palestine have been collected together in what is called the '*Apocrypha*' (from the Greek, meaning 'hidden' or secret, and so of uncertain authority.

The Apocrypha contains the following books:

1 and 2 Esdras	The Letter of Jeremiah
Tobit	The Prayer of Azariah and the
Judith	Song of the Three Young Men
Additions to Esther	Susanna
The Wisdom of Solomon	Bel and the Dragon
Ecclesiaticus, or the Wisdom of	The Prayer of Manasseh
Jesus son of Sirach	1 and 2 Maccabees
Baruch	

Some Bibles (including the RSV Ecumenical Edition) contain the Apocrypha as a separate collection of books, usually between the Old Testament and the New Testament. Other Bibles include the Apocryphal books among the books of the Old Testament as in the Jewish Scriptures (e.g. they have Tobit and Judith before Esther, and Baruch

'Early Christians were deeply impressed by the way God's promises in the Jewish Scriptures were fulfilled, as Jesus had claimed, in His death as well as His life, and the New Testament is full of quotations from the Old Testament.' This present-day Rabbi in Israel, and the boy he is preparing to take part in Scripture-reading and prayers, will read the same Scriptures from the massive decorated scroll standing beside them. But Jewish people do not accept Jesus' claims: they are still waiting for their Messiah.

The extract shown is part of the Book of Leviticus from an early 10th-century Hebrew MS of the Pentateuch.

86

after Lamentations). Many Bibles do not include the books of the Apocrypha at all. Broadly speaking, Protestant Churches accept as Scripture those books that were written in Hebrew and accepted by the Palestinian rabbis. The Roman Catholics and some Anglican Churches follow the tradition of the early Church, and accept the whole of the Septuagint as Scripture.

SCRIPTURE FULFILLED

NEW TESTAMENT QUOTATIONS FROM THE OLD TESTAMENT

According to the Gospel writers Jesus seems to have quoted from the Septuagint. Since Jesus was a Palestinian Jew, we should expect Him to have quoted the Scripture in Hebrew, or possibly in the Aramaic of the Targums.

The Gospel writers wrote their accounts of Jesus in Greek. They were writing for Christians who were either Gentiles or Jews of the Dispersion, and they all spoke Greek. When they quoted from the Old Testament they often quoted from the Septuagint. We have already noticed Luke's story of Jesus reading from the scroll in the synagogue at Nazareth. Jesus read from the Hebrew. However, Luke quotes the Greek of the Septuagint: 'He sent me to proclaim release to the captives and recovering of sight to the blind' (Luke 4.18, quoting Isaiah 61.1). If we look up this passage in Isaiah we do not find any mention of the blind recovering their sight. This is one of the passages where the Septuagint is different from the Hebrew. It does not make any difference to the sense of the story, but it does explain why we cannot always find the exact quotation when we look in our Old Testament, which is a translation of the Hebrew.

There is another reason why it is sometimes difficult to find the exact verse when we look up an Old Testament reference. The New Testament writers often quoted from memory, and sometimes they mixed up their quotations. Mark began his Gospel with a quotation:

'2. As it is written in Isaiah the prophet,

"Behold, I send my messenger before thy face,
who shall prepare thy way;
3. the voice of one crying in the wilderness:
Prepare the way of the Lord,
make his paths straight –"' (Mark 1.2–3).

Verse 3 is a quotation from Isaiah 40.3, but verse 2 is not from Isaiah at all. It is a quotation from Malachi 3.1.

OLD TESTAMENT IDEAS IN THE NEW TESTAMENT

We have seen that Jesus and the early Christians frequently quoted from the Old Testament, but the Old Testament was far more to them than a source of quotations. Because they were Jews and had been taught the Scriptures since they were children their whole way of thinking was influenced by the Old Testament.

OLD TESTAMENT PICTURES

Much of the picture-language which Jesus used comes from the Old Testament. He spoke about sheep and shepherds and said that He was the good shepherd (Matt. 25.32; Luke 15.4; John 10.11). Both images occur often in the Old Testament (e.g. Psalm 23, Ezekiel 37.24ff). In Jesus' parable of the wicked tenants and His allegory of the vine He was using Old Testament pictures (Mark 12.1–11; John 15.1–6; cf. Isa. 5.1–7; see also Vol. 1, p. 41).

The Revelation is a book with very few direct quotations from the Old Testament, but the whole book is full of Old Testament ideas and pictures. For example, when we read Revelation chapter 6 we do not find any Old Testament quotation, or any mention of Scripture, but the cross-references refer us to ten different Old Testament books. John's picture of the four horses and their riders has parallels with the picture in Zechariah of four chariots and their horses. The pictures are not the same, but probably John's vision of the horses was influenced by Zechariah's writing, perhaps without John himself even being aware of it. John's description of the Day of the Lord seems to have been influenced by his knowledge of Hosea. John describes everyone, from the greatest to the least, hiding in caves and calling on the mountains and rocks to hide them: 'Fall on us and hide us from the face of him who is seated on the throne' (Rev. 6.16). We find similar words in Hosea: 'And they shall say to the mountains, Cover us, and to the hills, Fall upon us' (Hosea 10.8).

OLD TESTAMENT PEOPLE

The New Testament contains many references to characters from the Old Testament, e.g. 'Woe to them! For they walk in the way of Cain, and abandon themselves for the sake of gain to Balaam's error, and perish in Korah's rebellion' (Jude 11). From Jude's letter we learn that some 'ungodly persons' had come into the Church: 'These men in their dreamings defile the flesh, reject authority, and revile the glorious ones' (Jude 4,8). Jude refers to them in terms of Cain, Balaam and Korah, three men who appear as wrong-doers in the Old Testament books of Genesis and Numbers. Cain murdered his brother (Gen. 4.3–8), Balaam was paid by the King of Moab to curse the children of Israel (Num. 22), Korah led a rebellion against Moses, and the ground opened up and swallowed him and his followers (Num. 16). Jude and his readers knew these stories so well that Jude could refer to them without any further explanation.

Jesus often referred to Old Testament characters. He spoke of the glory of Solomon (Matt. 6.29). He talked about all the murders that were written about in the Old Testament, from Cain's murder of Abel to the murder of Zechariah (Luke 11.50). When the Pharisees and Sadducees asked Him for a sign, He said the only sign they would be given was the sign of Jonah (Matt. 16.1–4).

OLD TESTAMENT CONCEPTS

All the great ideas of the New Testament have their roots in the Old Testament. We can only come to a deeper understanding of the New Testament by studying the Old Testament. For example, Jesus said, 'This cup is the new covenant in my blood' (1 Cor. 11.25). We cannot understand what He meant by 'blood' or by 'covenant' unless we study the Old Testament.

Some of the New Testament statements about the blood of Jesus seem very strange to twentieth-century people. The writer of 1 John says that 'the blood of Jesus . . . cleanses us from all sin' (1 John 1.7). The writer of Revelation speaks of those who have washed their garments in the blood of the lamb and made them white (Rev. 7.14). The study of the Old Testament shows us what blood meant to the Jews. We discover the importance of blood in the Jewish sacrificial system, and how some sacrifices were intended to remove sin.

One use of blood in the Old Testament was to 'seal the covenant'. 'Moses took the blood and threw it upon the people and said, "Behold the blood of the covenant which the LORD has made with you in accordance with all these words" (Exod. 24.8). The writer of Exodus was describing the covenant made at Mount Sinai, when God established a special relationship with the people of Israel. God promised to be their God, and the Israelites promised to keep God's law. Through the centuries that followed, the Israelites failed to keep the law, and so broke the covenant, but Jeremiah prophesied that God would make a new covenant with His people (Jer. 31.31). All these ideas and more lie behind the words of Jesus at the last supper: 'This cup is the new covenant in my blood'.

SCRIPTURE FULFILLED

We have seen that the task of the early Church was to proclaim what God had done in Jesus. One of the characteristics of the kerygma was the statement that Scripture had been fulfilled, for example, 'And he began to say to them, "Today this scripture has been fulfilled in your hearing" ' (Luke 4.21). In Jesus, God had done what He had promised through His prophets long ago.

1. IN THE TEACHING OF JESUS

According to Luke, Jesus claimed that Isaiah's prophecy had been fulfilled in Himself. He was thinking of words spoken by the same prophet when He said to the disciples of John the Baptist: 'Go, and tell John what you hear and see: the blind receive their sight and the lame walk, lepers are cleansed and the deaf hear, and the dead are raised up, and the poor have the good news preached to them' (Matt. 11.4–5).

Jesus taught that 'the Son of man also came not to be served but to serve, and to give his life as a ransom for many' (Mark 10.45). When Jesus called Himself 'Son of man' He was using another Old Testament idea. He saw Himself as the fulfilment of the Old Testament.

2. IN THE EARLY CHURCH

After Pentecost the disciples looked back at the life of Jesus and saw that it all fitted in with what they read in the Old Testament. For example, Moses had prophesied that God would raise up a prophet like him (Deut. 18.15–16). Peter claimed that Jesus was that prophet (Acts 3.22ff.).

Some of the prophets had predicted that God would send His anointed one, the Messiah. The first Christians proclaimed that Jesus was the Messiah, the Christ (Acts 5.42). They used this title for Jesus so much that it became part of His name – 'Jesus Christ'. Other titles which they used for Jesus also came from the Old Testament: e.g. the Lord (2 Peter 1.2), the Word of God (John 1.1) the High Priest (Heb. 4.14), the Lamb of God (Rev. 5.6).

The early Christians saw that Scripture had not only been fulfilled in Jesus. They saw Scripture also being fulfilled in the life of the early Church. The gift of the Spirit at Pentecost was a fulfilment of prophecy (Acts 2.17ff. cf. Joel 2.28ff.). The Spirit of Jesus in the Church meant that the good news was still being preached. Lame men were healed, and the dead were raised to life (Luke 7.22 cf. Acts 3.1–10; 9.36–41).

A NEW INTERPRETATION

1. BY JESUS

'He [Jesus] said to them, "O foolish men, and slow of heart to believe all that the prophets have spoken! Was it not necessary that the Christ should suffer these things and enter into his glory?" And beginning with Moses and all the prophets, he interpreted to them in all the scriptures the things concerning himself' (Luke 24.25–27). The Jews did not expect that the Messiah would suffer and die. However, according to

Luke Jesus taught the disciples that all through the Jewish Scriptures there were hints that the one whom God sent would have to suffer. According to this interpretation the events of the crucifixion were a part of God's plan. But Jews still do not accept Jesus' interpretation of the Old Testament.

Jesus took Old Testament verses which no one had ever thought of as being about the Messiah and applied them to Himself; for example, He took a verse from Hosea: 'On the third day he will raise us up' (Hos. 6.2; cf. Luke 24.46). He spoke of Himself as the stone which the builders had rejected (Ps 118.22; cf. Mark 12.10), and as the true vine (Ps. 80.8–15; cf. John 15.1).

2. BY JESUS' FOLLOWERS

The first Christians understood that Jesus was everything that Israel ought to have been. Israel ought to have obeyed God, but failed to do so. Jesus 'became obedient unto death, even death on a cross' (Phil. 2.8). Israel ought to have been a light to the nations (Isa. 60.2–3), but failed to be. Jesus was 'the light of the world' (John 8.12), and 'a light for the revelation of the Gentiles' (Luke 2.32).

If Jesus was the true Israel, then His followers were members of Israel, whether or not they were Jews by birth. Christians therefore thought of themselves as the New Israel. James addressed his letter to 'the twelve tribes in the dispersion' (see Vol. 1, p. 108), and Paul argued that the true descendants of Abraham were those who had faith like Abraham (see Gal. 3.7). For Paul 'the Israel of God' meant all those who believed in Jesus and followed Him: 'For neither circumcision counts for anything, nor uncircumcision, but a new creation. Peace and mercy be upon all who walk by this rule, upon the Israel of God' (Gal. 6.16).

STUDY SUGGESTIONS

WORDS AND MEANINGS

1. Explain the meaning of the following words:
   (a) Targums (b) Septuagint (c) Apocrypha (d) *genizah*
2. What is the relationship between the *Torah* and the *Pentateuch*?
3. What do the words 'major' and 'minor' mean when applied to books of prophecy in the Old Testament?
4. Explain the meaning of 'covenant' as it is used in the Old Testament.

REVIEW OF CONTENT

5. Give four names or expressions which the New Testament writers used to mean the Old Testament.

6. Which part of the Old Testament is most important to Jews?
7. Explain why the Jews classed the book of Kings as a 'prophet'.
8. Explain why the Septuagint was the 'Bible' of the early Church.

BIBLE STUDY

9. Look up Matthew 1.23. Use the cross-reference system to find this quotation in the Old Testament. What important difference is there between Matthew's quotation and the original Old Testament passage? How would you account for this difference?
10. Compare the four living creatures in Revelation 4.7 with the four living creatures in Ezekiel 1.5–10. Make a note of the things that are similar and the things that are different in the two visions.
11. Read the following verses, and say which Old Testament people Jesus was talking about in each case.
    (a) Matt. 22.31–32   (b) Mark 3.25–26   (c) Luke 4.25–27
    (d) John 8.37ff.
12. Use a concordance to find an Old Testament reference for each of the following ideas in the New Testament:
    (a) 'Behold the lamb of God' (John 1.29).
    (b) 'We have a great high priest' (Heb. 4.14).
    (c) 'The desolating sacrilege' (Mark 13.14).
    (d) 'Jesus found a young ass and sat on it' (John 12.14).
    (e) 'a chosen race, a royal priesthood' (1 Peter 2.9).
    (f) 'sealed . . . upon their foreheads' (Rev. 7.3).

FURTHER STUDY AND DISCUSSION

13. What should Christians do with Bibles that are old and worn out?
14. Which Old Testament book do you yourself value most highly, and for what reasons?
15. Which, if any, of the Churches in your country encourage their members to read the Apocrypha, or prescribe it for reading in Church services? Does your own Church do so? If so, which of the Aprocryphal books do you think are the most useful for Christians to study, and for what reasons? Do you think *all* Christians should read the Apocrypha?
16. Some Asian and African Church leaders claim that the traditional religions and scriptures of their own countries were 'given' by God as a preparation for the coming of the gospel to them, just as the religion of Israel and the Jewish Scriptures were a preparation for the coming of Jesus to the Church in Europe and the Near East. Do any of the Churches in your country make such claims? What is your own opinion in this matter?

7
The Canon: Christian Writings Become 'Scripture'

DOCUMENTS OF THE EARLY CHURCH

MANY BOOKS WRITTEN

The early Christians wrote many other Letters, Gospels, Apocalypses and Acts besides the twenty-seven books that we have in the New Testament. Some of the books that they wrote are still in existence. Some are mentioned by other early writers, so that we know they did exist, even though no copies seem to have survived. Eusebius, bishop of Caesarea from about AD315–340, wrote a history of the Church from the time of Jesus up to his own day. He quoted from many other writers (e.g. Papias), and gave the names of books which the Christians of his day used to read. Probably many other books have disappeared without leaving any trace. A modern way of describing early Christian books which are not in the New Testament is to call them 'apocryphal' or 'non-canonical' (see p. 97).

SOME OTHER DOCUMENTS

1. LETTERS

1 and 2 Clement: Clement was a leader of the Church in Rome. He wrote *1 Clement* to the Church in Corinth at the end of the first century or the beginning of the second century AD. He wrote to warn the Corinthian Christians of the dangers of divisions in the Church, and to encourage them to hold on to the Christian virtues. *2 Clement* is a sermon in the form of a letter, probably written by someone else.

The Letter of Barnabas: A letter which Barnabas may have written. In it the writer attacks the Jewish religion. It is clear that the letter was written after the fall of Jerusalem in AD70.

Seven Letters of Ignatius: Ignatius was a Christian leader in Antioch. In about AD107 he was taken by a guard of ten soldiers to Rome to die as a martyr. On his journey he wrote letters to the Churches of Ephesus, Magnesia, Tralles, Rome, Philadelphia and Smyrna. He also wrote to Polycarp, leader of the Church in Smyrna. Polycarp had the letters copied out, and sent the whole collection to the Church in Philippi.

The Preaching of Peter: A work which was very popular in the early Church. The writer wanted to show the superiority of the Christian religion. It was probably not written until the early second century.

2. A HANDBOOK

The Didache of the Twelve Apostles was an early Christian handbook about morals and Christian practice. It may have been compiled over many years, just as the Gospels probably were. Some of the sayings of Jesus which are found in the *Didache* are very similar to the sayings which we find in the Sermon on the Mount (Matt. 5–7). There are instructions about baptism, fasting, prayer, the Eucharist, and about the correct way to treat prophets, bishops and deacons.

3. OTHER GOSPELS

Many other Gospels were written besides the four which we have in the New Testament. Most of them were written long after Jesus died, and were later condemned as containing false teaching. Eusebius tells us that Jewish Christians liked the Gospel according to the Hebrews, a Gospel which we know that other Christian leaders knew and valued. Among the many other Gospels which existed were the Gospels of Philip, James, Peter, Thomas, and the Gospel of Truth. Some apocryphal Gospels we call 'infancy Gospels' because they only contain stories about Jesus' birth and childhood.

4. OTHER APOCALYPSES

In the second century AD three apocalypses were popular. One was the Revelation of John. The other two were:

The Shepherd of Hermas, written by Hermas, a freed slave in Rome. The book is an account of a series of visions which he received. In one of the visions there appeared an angel disguised as a shepherd, so the book was called *The Shepherd*.

The Apocalypse of Peter claims to have been written by Peter. It describes how Jesus gave the apostles a vision of their brothers and sisters in heaven, and tells of the rewards which they enjoy there.

5. OTHER ACTS

Many books of Acts were written, mostly in the second century or later. There were the Acts of Peter, the Acts of Paul, Acts of Andrew, the Acts of John and the Acts of Thomas as well.

THE IMPORTANCE OF THE SPOKEN WORD: A LIVING LINK WITH JESUS

We have seen how writing was a 'second-best' for the early Christians. Church leaders wrote letters when they were unable to visit people (see Vol. 1. pp. 75–76, 86). They wrote Gospels because the Church was growing fast and it had become impossible to give personal teaching to all the new leaders and preachers. There were two things on which the

Early Christians did place a high value: the Old Testament and the link they had with Jesus through the apostles.

The apostles had known Jesus better than anyone else. While they lived they were able to share their first-hand knowledge of Jesus with others. When the apostles died there were still plenty of people who had known them. Papias (see pp. 23 and 77) wrote that whenever anyone came to him who had been a follower of the apostles, he asked him about the apostles, what Andrew or Peter had said, or Philip or Thomas or James or John, or Matthew or any other disciple of the Lord, and what any disciples of the Lord were still saying. He did not think that things out of books would be as helpful to him as the words 'of a living and abiding voice'.

When those who had known the apostles died, there were still the people who had known *them*. Irenaeus (Bishop of Lyons, c.AD175–222) said that he too had known someone who had known the apostles. When he was a child he had known Polycarp, bishop of Smyrna. Irenaeus wrote: 'Polycarp constantly taught those things which he had learned from the apostles, which are also the traditions of the Church, which alone are true.' Both Papias and Polycarp were proud of the living link they had with Jesus. We might put it in a diagram like this:

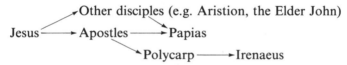

Probably the facts were far less simple than such a diagram suggests. However, it is clear from what Papias and Irenaeus wrote that they valued the spoken word. It helped them to know that their information was good and the witnesses were reliable.

CHRISTIAN WRITINGS BECOME SCRIPTURE

'Scripture is right in saying "First of all believe that God is one, the maker and builder of all things" ' (Irenaeus, quoted by Eusebius).

Irenaeus quoted 'Scripture', but the verse he quotes comes from the *Shepherd of Hermas*. Clearly Irenaeus considered that the *Shepherd of Hermas* was Scripture. However, we have not got Hermas in our New Testament and we do not think of it as Scripture. How is it that some early Christian writings came to be thought of as Scripture and others did not?

The process which led to some books being accepted as Scripture and other books being rejected is called the 'formation of the canon'. 'Canon' was a Greek word which originally meant a measuring rod, and came later to mean a list. When we speak of the 'canon' of the New Testament we mean the list of twenty-seven books which we recognize as Scripture. The books included in that list can be described as 'canonical'. 'Canonical Gospels' are the Gospels we have in the New Testament. Other Gospels are called 'non-canonical' or 'apocryphal'.

The formation of the canon was not a formal process or an organized movement. It happened in different ways in different places.

THE FIRST LIST—MARCION

Marcion (died c.AD160) was the first Christian to make his own list of the Christian books which he accepted as Scripture. However, he and his teaching were condemned by the rest of the Church as heretical. Marcion rejected the whole of the Old Testament. He believed that the God of the Old Testament was not the same as the God of love revealed by Jesus. Marcion also rejected most of the letters and Gospels written by Jesus' followers. He thought that they were too Jewish. The only books which Marcion accepted as Scripture were ten letters of Paul and part of the Gospel according to Luke. Marcion's list had less than half the books of our New Testament.

DEFENCE AGAINST MARCION

Marcion was a gifted leader and many Christians followed him. The other Church leaders disagreed with his teaching, but they found themselves in a difficult position. In earlier arguments against false teaching they had used the Old Testament to support their views. But Marcion did not accept the Old Testament, so they had to find new ways of arguing with him and defending the truth.

Irenaeus wrote a long book called *Against All Heresies*. Marcion had refused to accept the teaching of any of the apostles except Paul and his friend Luke. Irenaeus argued firmly that *all* the apostles were witnesses to the truth. He said that there had to be four Gospels, just as there were four winds, and four corners of the earth. Irenaeus quoted from many Christian writings which he called 'Scripture'.

Clement of Alexandria (see p. 23) was writing at about the same time as Irenaeus. Clement also quoted the letters of the apostles as Scripture, and included the following books in Scripture: the *Letter of Barnabas*, *1 Clement* and the *Preaching of Peter*.

It seems as if the Christians of that period were collecting and using as many Christian books as possible. Marcion had taught that only a very few books were Scripture, but other Christians reacted against his teaching by using a great many books. People like Irenaeus believed that though the books were different from each other, they were all witness to the same Christ and to the same truth which Christ had revealed.

In the writing of Irenaeus and Clement we notice two interesting facts:

1. There was no agreed name for these Christian writings except 'Scripture'.

2. At that time many Christians accepted as 'Scripture' more books than we do now.

MONTANISM — A NEW PROBLEM

Montanus was a preacher in Asia Minor who foretold that the new Jerusalem would come very soon. He began a revival movement in the Church, a movement which was named after him — Montanism. Montanism flourished during the second half of the second century AD.

Montanus and his followers proclaimed that God had poured out His Spirit upon them in a new way, to prepare for the return of Jesus. They not only preached this message, but also wrote down their visions and prophecies, and the stories of their martyrs. They claimed that just as the Holy Spirit had produced the Old Testament and the Christian writings of the apostles, so He was now inspiring them to write Scripture. When they met for worship they read their own books alongside the Jewish Scriptures and the new Christian Scriptures.

DEFENCE AGAINST MONTANISM

Montanus raised a big question for the Christians of his day. Was it possible that the books written by Montanus and his friends were as valuable as the writings of apostles like Peter, John and Paul? Montanus and his followers said that their books were inspired by the Holy Spirit. How could anyone judge whether or not a book was inspired by the Holy Spirit? The Montanists read their books in Church worship. Which books were suitable for reading in public worship?

The Church had to decide which books were Scripture and which were not.

THE GUIDELINES

Gradually Christians worked out that in order to be classed as Scripture a book had to meet certain conditions.

1. The book must be *an ancient book*. None of the Montanist writings were ancient, so none of them could be Scripture.

2. The book must have been *written by an apostle or the friend of an apostle*. Hermas was neither an apostle nor the friend of an apostle, so the *Shepherd of Hermas* could not be thought of as Scripture. Mark and Luke were not apostles, but each of them had been the close friend of an apostle, so their books were accepted.

A lot of writings were questioned on this basis. For example, no one knew who had written the *Letter to the Hebrews*. Some scholars

'In deciding which books to accept as Scripture the Church gave priority to those written by the apostles, who had known Jesus, or by friends of the apostles. But it was some time before agreement was reached.' A 6th-century mosaic of St Lawrence, a deacon martyred in 268, shows a cupboard with the four 'canonical' Gospels from which the saint would have read at the Eucharist, as deacons do today.

thought that Paul had written it, so they considered it to be Scripture. Others were sure that Paul had not written it, and thought that it probably was not Scripture. Hebrews became one of the 'disputed books', and for a time Christian writers in the West stopped using it as Scripture. (In this context 'the West' usually means those places where people spoke Latin. The Eastern Churches were Greek-speaking.)

3. A book must be *orthodox in its teaching*. No book which contained false teaching could be Scripture. Some books were clearly heretical: the *Gospel of Philip*, the *Gospel of Thomas* and the *Gospel of Truth* were all rejected as heretical Gospels.

The Montanists taught that the Paraclete, the 'Counsellor', whom Jesus had promised according to John, had come in their spirit of prophecy. Some people were so suspicious of Montanism that they even came to doubt whether John's Gospel was Scripture.

4. A book must be *suitable for reading in public worship*. When Christians met together for worship they read their Christian books as well as the Old Testament.

5. A book must be *generally accepted by the Church* and its leaders. (This is something like the Muslim doctrine of *Ijma*: when a community guided by God is in agreement, then the opinion at which they have arrived is a guidance from God.) Some books which had been accepted were no longer acceptable. There were three apocalyptic books which had been widely read by Christians. However, most Montanist writings were apocalyptic, so people became doubtful about all apocalypses. The writers of the apocalypses claimed that they had been directly inspired, but so did Montanist writers. In the end the Revelation of John was the only apocalypse to be accepted, and for a long time Christians in the East doubted whether even that should be counted as Scripture. (We consider the question of inspiration more fully in Special Note B. p. 106.)

The last of these guidelines is very vague. It is not an absolute standard of judgement, but rather a sort of compromise – 'as long as we all agree that this book is Scripture, then it is so'. The Revelation of John, whose writer makes no claim to be an apostle or the friend of an apostle, and which may have been written late, was eventually accepted as Scripture. So was Hebrews, in spite of the fact that no one knew who had written it. The Letter of Barnabas was ancient, written by a friend of the apostles, and did not contain false teaching, yet the Church did not accept it as Scripture. The Didache and 1 Clement were also rejected. Some Christians believe that the list of those books which were accepted as Scripture and are now in our Bible was given directly to the leaders of the Church by God. This view raises the question, to *which* leaders did God give the list?

99

THE NAMING OF THE NEW TESTAMENT

For a long time Christians had no special name for their collection of Scriptures. They were treated as 'Scripture', but the Jewish sacred writings were also 'Scripture'. When Irenaeus wanted to refer to the Christian writings he had no name for them. He was forced to speak of 'the Four-fold Gospel' or 'the Letters of the Apostle'.

Jews often called their Scriptures 'the Law'. Christians might have called their Scriptures 'the Gospel', but 'Gospel' had already come to mean one particular kind of book. Some early Christian writers spoke of the Jewish Scriptures as 'the Prophets' and called the Christian Scriptures 'the Apostles'. Those seem very suitable names but they were never widely used.

At the end of the second century several writers developed the idea of two covenants. There was the old covenant which God had made with Israel, and the new covenant which He had made with the Church. In the Old Testament, Isaiah, Jeremiah and Ezekiel had all prophesied that God would make a new relationship with His people, and establish a new covenant (Isa. 55.3; Jer. 32.40; Ezek. 16.60). Paul had taken up this idea in his letters to Corinth and Galatia: 'Our sufficiency is from God, who has qualified us to be ministers of a new covenant, not in a written code but in the spirit' (2 Cor. 3.6; cf. Gal.4.24). More than a century passed before Christian writers began to develop the idea.

The Greek word for covenant was *'diatheke'*. It was used for a binding relationship, like a marriage or the adoption of a child. It also meant the documents that belonged to the relationship, e.g. the marriage certificate or the adoption certificate. When a Christian spoke of the 'new covenant' it meant the new relationship which God had established with the Church through Jesus. It could also mean the documents of that relationship, the Christian Scriptures.

Christians began to call their collection of Christian Scriptures 'The New Covenant'. Naturally they called the Jewish Scriptures 'The Old Covenant'. The names fitted perfectly, for several reasons:

1. The names showed that the two collections of Scripture were closely related to each other, that they belonged together. They asserted that anyone like Marcion who rejected the Jewish Scriptures was wrong.

2. The names showed that in some way the Christian Church had replaced Judaism. God's promise of a new covenant had come true through Jesus.

3. The documents of a relationship are always less important than the relationship itself. The most important thing for Christians is the relationship which Jesus makes between His followers and God. The name 'New Covenant' describe the relationship as well as the documents.

From the second century onwards most Christians in Europe and North Africa spoke Latin. Translated into Latin '*diatheke*' becomes '*testamentum*', from which we get our names 'Old Testament' and 'New Testament'.

Together the Old and New Testaments make 'the Bible' or 'Scripture' for Christians. By the end of the third century AD all Christians knew that Scripture had two parts, which they called the Old Covenant and the New Covenant.

A SPONTANEOUS MOVEMENT

For three hundred years after Jesus died, Christians were a small minority. Their religion was illegal and they were often persecuted, although some of the Roman Emperors were more tolerant than others. But by AD324 Constantine the Great had won control of the whole of the Roman Empire. He became a Christian and for the first time the Christian religion received encouragement from the ruling authorities. By the time of Constantine the contents of the New Testament and its name had already been fixed.

We should be wrong if we imagined that the Church leaders had settled these matters by calling conferences and councils. None of the great ecumenical councils of the Church happened before the reign of Constantine. There had been some councils in North Africa, but normally every bishop made his own decisions. He might have had the opportunity of meeting with some other bishops and then he would have discussed the problems that his Church was facing. He might have written letters to ask what the Church was doing in other areas. But it was up to him and his Church leaders to decide what should be done in his area and which books they considered to be suitable for reading in worship.

SURVIVING LISTS

A few lists which were made in the early centuries AD have survived, and we shall take a brief look at them.

1. THE MURATORIAN CANON (BOOKS ACCEPTED IN ROME)

In about AD200 a theologian who lived in Rome made a list of books. It may have been a private list rather than an official one. It was discovered by Cardinal Muratori, and it is not complete, so that it is often called the 'Muratorian Fragment'. The beginning and the end of the list are missing, but in spite of that it tells us a great deal about which books the Roman Church accepted at the end of the second century. There are four New Testament books which are not included on the list: Hebrews, James, and 1 and 2 Peter. The Apocalypse of Peter is on the list. The writer says that the Shepherd of Hermas could be read, but not in public worship. He also lists two books which he says were forgeries and should not be read at all: the Letter to Laodicea and the Letter to the Alexandrians.

2. ATHANASIUS'S EASTER LETTER (BOOKS ACCEPTED IN ALEXANDRIA)

In AD367 Athanasius, Bishop of Alexandria, wrote a letter to the Churches in his area. In the letter he listed all the books of the New Testament. He also mentioned the Shepherd of Hermas and the Didache of the Twelve Apostles. Athanasius said that these two books were useful for instruction although they were not part of the canon.

3. EUSEBIUS'S HISTORY OF THE CHURCH (BOOKS ACCEPTED IN CAESAREA)

Eusebius, Bishop of Caesarea, wrote a history of the Church at the beginning of the third century. He put the Christian writings into four groups:

(a) '*Recognized Books*', which everyone accepted: Four Gospels, Acts, the Letters of Paul, Hebrews, 1 Peter, 1 John and Revelation (if an apostle had written it).

(b) '*Disputed Books*', which nevertheless everyone knew and read: James, Jude, 2 Peter, 2 and 3 John.

(c) '*Spurious Books*', which were not written by an apostle, but which most Christians knew: The Acts of Paul, The Shepherd of Hermas, the Letter of Barnabas, The Didache of the Twelve Apostles, The Apocalypse of Peter, Revelation (if it was *not* written by an apostle), and the Gospel according to the Hebrews. Eusebius did not like Revelation, but he knew that earlier Church leaders had liked it, and regarded it as apostolic.

(d) '*Heretical Books*', which were not accepted by any Churchmen and should be 'thrown out as impious and beyond the pale'; the Gospel of Peter, the Gospel of Thomas, the Gospel of Matthias, the Acts of Andrew, the Acts of John, the Acts of Peter and the Preaching of Peter.

4. THE COUNCIL OF CARTHAGE (BOOKS ACCEPTED IN AFRICA)

In 397 a council met at Carthage in North Africa. It produced a list of books which the Churches in Africa accepted as canonical. At that time they accepted the twenty-seven books which we have in the New Testament.

5. THE VULGATE

The people of Western Europe and North Africa spoke Latin. Since Christians wanted to read the Scriptures in a language which they could

In AD 382 the Pope commissioned the scholar Jerome to make a revised Latin translation of the Bible known as the Vulgate, which was used throughout the Western Church for a thousand years. This page of a beautifully decorated and illustrated Psalter of the 15th century shows Jerome reading.

understand, they had translated the books of the New Testament into Latin. In 382 the Bishop of Rome asked a biblical scholar called Jerome to make a revised Latin translation of the whole Bible.

Jerome began with the New Testament, and it took him twenty-two years to complete his work. His translation was called the 'Vulgate', which meant that it was the official public edition (in Latin, *'editio vulgata'*). The Vulgate came to be used everywhere in the Western Church, and for a thousand years it was the only Bible that Western Christians knew.

Jerome had his private doubts about some of the New Testament books. He did not believe that Paul had written Hebrews. He was not certain that 2 and 3 John, Jude, 2 Peter, James or Revelation were Scripture. However, the Bishop told him to include all twenty-seven books and he did so. We have read them as Scriptures ever since. (Jerome also knew that the Jews did not accept all the books of the Septuagint as Scripture. However, the Bishop told him to translate all the books which Christians were used to reading as Scripture, so the Vulgate includes the books of the Apocrypha.)

Apart from these lists which have survived we cannot be sure what decisions were made in different Churches at different times. It is quite possible that a Christian leader in Antioch made a list in AD150 of the books which the Antiochene Church read as Scripture; but if he did, the list disappeared long ago. Perhaps a Church secretary in Lyons did the same thing; but if so, that list has gone too. All that we have from Lyons is some of the writings of Irenaeus, Bishop of Lyons. From studying what Irenaeus wrote we get some idea of what books he accepted as Scripture.

From the surviving lists we can see that Churches in different countries eventually came to the same decisions about which books were Scripture and which were not. When Christians in the West accepted the Vulgate as the official Bible there was no more discussion on the matter. In the sixteenth century Martin Luther considered that the Letter of James was of less worth than John, Romans or 1 Peter. He complained that it did not preach Christ and called it 'a letter of straw'; but he still accepted it as Scripture.

STUDY SUGGESTIONS

WORDS AND MEANINGS

1. Explain the meaning of the following words as used in this chapter:
   (a) canonical   (b) covenant   (c) heretical
2. Would you describe Greece as being in the 'West' or in the 'East' in the context of:

(a) the second century AD?

(b) the twentieth century AD?

3. Explain the difference between a 'private' list and an 'official' list, as relating to the books which the Churches accept as Scripture.

REVIEW OF CONTENT

4. For each of the following types of writing, give examples of two non-canonical books:

   (a) Gospels (b) Letters (c) Acts (d) Apocalypses

5. Which groups of Churches were uncertain whether the following books were Scripture?

   (a) The Letter to the Hebrews (b) The Revelation of John?

6. Give an example of a human relationship which can be described as a 'covenant relationship'.

7. 'The names fitted perfectly.' Explain what was gained by giving the names 'Old Covenant' and 'New Covenant' to the Jewish and the Christian collections of Scripture.

8. What historical connection did Irenaeus claim to have with Jesus?

9. (a) Name two people who accepted *more* than 27 Christian books as Scripture.

   (b) Name one person who accepted *less* than 27 Christian books as Scripture.

10. For what reason can a book by a modern writer never be accepted as Scripture?

11. What are the five important lists of canonical books which have survived? In each case give its approximate date, and say which Church or Churches accepted that list.

FURTHER STUDY AND DISCUSSION

12. How far can it be said that there was any fixed standard by which the early Church judged whether or not a book was Scripture?

13. How important is it to believe that the Christians who selected books as Scripture were themselves inspired by Holy Spirit?

14. 'Marcion and his teaching were condemned by the rest of the Church as heretical.' Explain what this statement means. What teaching, if any, does your own Church describe as heretical?

15. Some Christians today argue that no Church should take a major decision about questions of belief or practice without consulting a world-wide, or at least a national, council of all the Churches. What is your opinion on the subject, in the light of what you have learnt about the formation of the canon of Christian 'Scripture'?

The Inspiration of the New Testament

'All scripture is inspired by God and profitable for teaching, for reproof, for correction, and for training in righteousness, that the man of God may be complete, equipped for every good work.' (2 Tim. 3.16)

In the RSV a footnote gives an alternative translation for the first seven words of this verse: '*Every scripture inspired by God is also . . .*' The Greek text is clear enough; a word-for-word translation would be: 'Every writing God-inspired is also profitable, etc.'. But what exactly did the writer mean by the words 'scripture' and 'God-inspired'? First, by 'scripture' he must mean the Old Testament, the Jewish 'scripture', because the New Testament did not yet exist when 2 Timothy was written. Secondly, 'God-inspired' must mean that God breathed His Spirit into it. The Greek word used meant both 'breath' or 'wind' and also 'spirit' (the literal meaning of the English word 'inspire' is 'breathe into').

So what do Christians today mean when they say that the Bible, and more especially the New Testament, is 'inspired'?

Different Churches vary in their attitudes towards the Bible and its inspiration or authority. Some Churches accept that the Bible writers were guided by the Holy Spirit, but they say that the Church existed before the Bible did, and so it has the right to interpret the teaching and meaning of Scripture in the light of up-to-date historical and linguistic research and scientific discovery. Others claim to be 'Bible-based', and say they are 'under the authority of Scripture'. Some teach that every word written by the Bible writers was directly inspired by God and must be understood as literally true.

Few if any Christians, however, would say that God actually 'spoke' the words of the New Testament while Mark, Paul, and the others wrote them down. We do not think of the New Testament writers as God's secretaries (in the way Muslims think of Muhammad receiving God's words through the Angel Gabriel, and some Jews still think of Moses writing down God's Law on Sinai). We do not believe the Bible is that sort of book – a 'magical set of unchangeable sounds', as the Indian theologian Mathew John has put it.

Christians believe that God 'spoke' by sending His Son and revealing Himself in Jesus (Vol. 1, p. 3). As we shall see more fully in chapter 8, our reading of the New Testament today is only possible because of a long process of compiling, writing, editing, copying and translating which has continued for nearly two thousand years. Simply to believe, for example, that John was 'inspired' to write down what he heard when Jesus said 'I am the light of the world', or 'the Father is in me and I am in the Father', or 'This I command you, to love one another', is not enough. We have to believe that at every stage God has been 'breathing His Spirit' into *all* the people whose work has brought those words of Jesus to us in our own language. What are those stages, and who were the people involved?

THE MANY STAGES OF INSPIRATION

JESUS AND HIS DISCIPLES

The New Testament writers tell us that Jesus Himself was filled with the Spirit, and gave the Spirit to His disciples. John's Gospel begins with the witness of John the Baptist: 'I saw the Spirit descend as a dove from heaven, and it remained on him ... this is he who baptizes with the Holy Spirit' (John 1.32–33). And it ends with the risen Jesus as He stood among His disciples: 'he breathed on them, and said to them, "Receive the Holy Spirit" ' (John 20.21).

Only Jesus has ever been completely filled with the Holy Spirit, but He promised that the Spirit would guide His disciples 'into all the truth' (John 16.3). When they remembered what Jesus had said and done, the Spirit was active in their memories. At Pentecost when the Spirit 'gave them utterance' in other tongues, those who repented and were baptized as a result of the disciples' preaching were themselves promised 'the gift of the Spirit' (Acts 2.1–11, 38–41).

EARLY COMPILERS, WRITERS AND EDITORS

We are accustomed to thinking of the evangelists and other New Testament writers as being inspired by God – but in what way do we think they were inspired?

According to Luke's account Paul, for example, was directly inspired by the voice of the risen Jesus to change the direction of his life, and after his baptism he put all his energy and enthusiasm into preaching and writing about Jesus (Acts 9.1–20). But there is no evidence that Paul thought of himself as writing 'God-inspired Scripture'. In fact he sometimes said he was only giving his own opinion. However, he did so 'as one who by the Lord's mercy is trustworthy' (1 Cor. 7.25). He knew that God's Spirit was at work in his life, guiding and directing him.

As time went on a number of people undertook to collect and record the accounts of what Jesus had said and done, as handed down orally by 'eyewitnesses and ministers of the word', just as the various Churches preserved the letters of Paul and others. And later still some of their work was revised and edited, to serve a particular purpose or special occasion. None of them expected their writing to become

Scripture. In many cases their individual human characteristics can be recognized, like Matthew's interest in legal affairs, Luke's concern for times and places, and James's emphasis on Christian *doing* as well as believing.

Without doubting, therefore, that compilers and writers worked in response to the call of the Spirit, we may decide that some passages in the New Testament – such as Paul's description of the nature of 'love' in 1 Corinthians 13 – are more Spirit-filled than others. Some passages we may take as true for the time when they were written, but not necessarily true for ours.

SCRIBES AND COPYISTS, COLLECTORS AND SELECTORS

Then came the turn of the scribes and copyists. They did not create the words of the New Testament, but the Spirit surely guided them to ensure that faithful copies should be available for all the Churches. Without their painstaking work we should not have the New Testament today. We may also believe that it was the Spirit who guided the early Christians to value what their leaders had written, to build up collections of books in centres of learning like Rome and Alexandria, and eventually to agree upon which books should be accepted as 'Scripture'. Throughout the Middle Ages too, before printing was invented, the mark of the Spirit is seen in the manuscripts beautifully decorated and illustrated by the monks who did the copying.

TRANSLATORS AND TEXTUAL SCHOLARS

Throughout the history of the Church Christians have had to trust in the work of translators. And however great their learning and understanding, all translators of Scripture depend upon the Holy Spirit to guide their choice of text and inspire them to make translations which carry the true meaning of the original (see ch. 8).

In more recent times the work of theologians and historians who study the biblical texts, and the discoveries of those who bring further ancient manuscripts to light, have greatly added to our understanding of the New Testament and its meaning. The scholars do not always agree in their conclusions, but most Christians would accept that their thinking and writing can serve as a channel through which the Holy Spirit speaks to us today (see ch. 8).

WE WHO READ

At the end of the line we come to ourselves as readers. The New Testament can be read as literature, history, or simply an interesting collection of ancient documents, without thinking of it as inspired by God at all. We could say that it is only inspired for those who love Jesus and want to do His will: 'If a man loves me, he will keep my word'

'As time went on people collected and recorded accounts of what Jesus had said and done, as handed down by eyewitnesses.' In many countries today scholars are recording the ancient beliefs and stories connected with the history of their peoples, like this young Chinese writer listening to the words of an elderly villager. Some theologians consider that such traditional beliefs can be seen as a preparation for the coming of the Gospel.

(John 14.23). Only people who are themselves filled with the Spirit will hear God speaking to them through the Bible.

The New Testament tells us about the man Jesus who lived nearly 2,000 years ago. Through the inspiration of the Holy Spirit it also enables us in our own lives to meet the risen Jesus who is Himself the Word of God, 'living and active, piercing to the division of soul and spirit, of joints and marrow, and discerning the thoughts and intentions of the heart' (Heb. 4.12).

STUDY SUGGESTIONS

WORDS AND MEANINGS

1. What do the words 'literal' and 'literally' mean in the following sentences?
   (a) The literal meaning of the word 'inspire' is 'breathe into'.
   (b) Some Christians say that every word in the Bible must be understood as literally true.

REVIEW OF CONTENT

2. (a) What does the word 'scripture' mean in 2 Tim. 3.16?
   (b) What does it *not* mean, and why not?
3. List *six* of the stages in the formation of the canon of Christian Scripture.
   At which stage or stages would you say that the inspiration of the Holy Spirit has been most important?

BIBLE STUDY

4. Would you consider the following passage as having been inspired (i) for all time, (ii) for the time of writing, or (iii) not at all?
   (a) Acts 15.28–29   (b) Eph. 2.11–22   (c) 1 Cor. 11.6
   (d) Gal. 2.28   (e) Gal. 5.12   Give your reasons in each case.

FURTHER STUDY AND DISCUSSION

5. How can we distinguish clearly between what is divinely inspired and what is only human, (a) in the work of Christian writers and teachers, and (b) in the motives and actions of Christian people?
6. What connection, if any, can you see between the statement that 'Only Jesus has ever been completely filled with the Spirit' (p. 107) and the Christian teaching that only Jesus is without sin?
7. Churches vary in their attitudes toward the Bible and its inspiration and authority. What is the attitude of your own Church in this matter? What is your own attitude, and for what reasons?

8

Texts and Translations

TEXTS

'^{k} Some of the most ancient authorities bring the book to a close at the end of verse 8. One authority concludes the book by adding after verse 8 the following: *But they reported briefly to Peter and those with him all that they had been told. And after this, Jesus himself sent out by means of them, from east to west, the sacred and imperishable proclamation of eternal salvation.* Other authorities include the preceding passage and continue with verses 9–20. In most authorities verses 9–20 follow immediately after verse 8; a few authorities insert additional material after verse 14.'

The above paragraph appears as a footnote at the very end of Mark's Gospel in the Revised Standard Version Ecumenical Edition, and nearly all modern Bibles include similar notes. A previous edition of the RSV ended Mark's Gospel at v. 8, with vv. 9–20 printed in italics as a separate footnote. The Good News Bible has vv. 9–20 in brackets with the heading 'An old ending to the Gospel^a', and a footnote '^{a} *Some manuscripts and ancient translations do not have this ending to the Gospel (verses 9–20).*' Because the ancient authorities of Mark's Gospel vary so much, most biblical scholars today think that vv. 9–20 were probably added to the original version.

We have already discussed the cross-references which are given in many Bibles (Vol. 1, p. 91), but until now we have not considered the footnotes. The footnotes are concerned with the actual words used in the text, and they are usually indicated by a letter, e.g. ^{a}. Most of them begin 'Other ancient authorities . . .', or 'Other texts and versions . . .' To understand what those 'ancient authorities' were, and why there are differences between them, we need to go back to the beginning and consider how the words which Mark or his scribe originally wrote have come down to us.

MANUSCRIPTS

A 'manuscript' is a book or a document written by hand. Nowadays it may be typewritten, but a typewriter is a modern invention. Even printing was not invented until the fifteenth century; before that time all books had to be copied out by hand. As we have seen, some of the New Testament writers may have done the actual writing of their books themselves, while others (e.g. Paul) used a scribe to write down their words for them. In either case the very first version they made is what we call the 'autograph manuscript'. It would be helpful to know exactly what Mark or Paul originally wrote, but the autograph manuscripts of the New Testament books do not exist any more. They wore out and fell to pieces many centuries ago. All that exist now are copies of copies. However, thousands of manuscripts of the New Testament do still exist. (The abbreviation for manuscript is MS, or for more than one, MSS.)

PAPYRUS SCROLLS

The New Testament writers wrote on papyrus (see Vol. 1, ch. 6). At first they used papyrus rolls or 'scrolls', both for the autograph MS and for making copies. They wrote without using punctuation.

From the beginning of the second century, Christians used codices instead of rolls. A codex ('codices' is the plural) was made like a modern exercise book. Sheets of papyrus were laid one on top of the other, fastened together in the middle, and folded over to make a book. A codex was much easier to handle than a roll, and in a codex the scribe could write on both sides of the papyrus, so that it could contain a lot more writing than a roll. It was possible to copy all four Gospels, or all the letters of Paul, on to one large papyrus codex. Codices were also easier to carry around. The twenty-seven books of the New Testament would have needed at least eight large rolls, which would have been very awkward to transport.

The best papyrus MSS of the New Testament were probably those which belonged to the Churches in the great cities, like Rome and Alexandria. It was in such cities that the Christians were most severely persecuted, and in the persecutions those copies of the New Testament books would have been destroyed. Papyrus was easily damaged anyway, especially if it got damp. It soon became worn out and the sheets of a codex fell apart. The only place where papyrus documents have survived is in Egypt where the climate is very dry. In recent times a number of papyrus MSS have been discovered there. Most of them are only small fragments, but there are 108 leaves of a codex which contained the Gospel of John, and 87 leaves of a codex containing Paul's letters. Scholars believe that both these MSS were copied out at the beginning of the third century. All papyrus MSS are very old; the most recent ones were made in c.AD600. The oldest piece to be discovered is a fragment containing five verses of John's Gospel. It is part of a codex that was made during the first half of the second century, possibly as early as AD130.

VELLUM CODICES

About the time when Constantine became the head of the Roman Empire a new material became fashionable for the best books. This was vellum, or parchment, made from the skins of young cattle, sheep or goats. The skin was scraped with pumice and polished with chalk. It was a beautiful material for writing on, and much stronger than papyrus. When Constantine ordered fifty copies of the Scriptures to be made for use in the churches of his new capital city, he said that the copies were to be made on vellum. From the writing of Jerome we know that in the library at Caesarea papyrus books which wore out were replaced by copies made on vellum.

Several vellum codices of the New Testament which were made in the fourth and fifth centuries still survive today. Manuscripts as old as that are very important, because they help us to get as close as possible to the words which Mark and Paul and the others originally wrote. As well as those very old MSS there are many more which are less old. There exist today about 4,000 MSS of parts of the Greek New Testament, about 8,000 MSS of the Latin Vulgate, and about 1,000 MSS of translations in other ancient languages, including Syriac, Coptic, Gothic, Georgian, Ethiopic, Arabic and Slavonic.

COPIES OF COPIES

When all books were copied out by hand each copy was slightly different. The scribe who was copying would make mistakes, especially if he was in a hurry. Even if he was taking great care he was almost certain to make a few mistakes. We all know how easy it is to copy something wrongly. Sometimes a whole line gets left out, or copied twice. Sometimes we add words that are not actually in the original. If one copyist made a mistake, then everyone who copied his copy was likely to make the same mistake. A later copyist might realize that a mistake had been made and try to correct it, but his correction might not be exactly what the first writer had written. The diagram below shows what can happen by the time an original document has been copied by a number of different people.

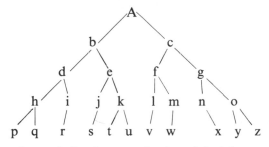

In the diagram A stands for Autograph, the original document; b and c are copies which were made from A; d and e were copied from b; f and g were copied from c. All the mistakes made in c are likely to be found in

113

f, g, l, m, n, o, v, w, x, y, and z. Suppose that only p, l, and y still exist. Not one of them will be exactly the same as A. None of them will be exactly the same as each other. We might think that l was an older copy and therefore closer to A. However, b might have been a very good copy, and c might have been a poor copy. In that case p may be closer to A than either l or y.

The job of textual scholars is to study the different copies which are available, and consider the evidence. People who can read Greek can use the footnotes in a Greek New Testament to find out exactly which MSS give the different texts.

PRINTED BIBLES

In Europe in the fifteenth and sixteenth centuries there was a great revival of learning. People became interested in mathematics and science, in the literature of earlier times, and in painting, sculpture and architecture. They re-discovered old ideas and invented new ones. This period is known as the 'Renaissance', which means re-birth. One of the new inventions was the printing press, which meant that books no longer needed to be copied out by hand. A printing press could quickly make thousands of identical copies, so new ideas spread faster than ever.

As a result, Christians began to ask questions about the Church, and about its early history and writings. There began the movement which we call the 'Reformation', which led to the Protestant Churches becoming separated from the Roman Catholic Church. Some of the questions which Christians were asking at that time were about the Bible. They asked why it was that everyone read the Bible in Latin. Ordinary people no longer spoke Latin. Christian scholars began to make new translations in the languages of the people. The first translators of the Bible had to translate from the Latin text, which was the earliest that they had. In 1516, however, a Dutch scholar named Erasmus published a Greek edition of the New Testament, and for the next 300 years all Protestant translators used a text based on Erasmus's Greek text. Roman Catholic scholars used the 'Complutensian Polyglot', an edition of the Bible published with the Pope's permission at about the same time as Erasmus's Greek New Testament. (It was called 'Complutensian' from 'Complutum', the Latin name for Alcalá in Spain where it was issued, and 'Polyglot' from a Greek word meaning 'many-tongued', because it contained the New Testament in Greek and Latin, and the Old Testament in Hebrew, Greek and Latin.)

RECENT DEVELOPMENTS

When Erasmus published the New Testament in Greek he used the MS texts which were available to him. The one which he used the most had

The very oldest piece of New Testament MS so far discovered is this papyrus fragment, from a copy of John's Gospel which may have been made within a hundred and fifty years of Jesus' death.

Following the Reformation, many Bible translations were based on the Greek text published by Erasmus in 1516.' This portrait of Erasmus at work was 'drawn from the life' by the famous German painter and engraver Albrecht Dürer.'

been made in the fifteenth century. Since the time of Erasmus several things have made a difference to the study of the text of the New Testament.

1. MORE MANUSCRIPTS

Two hundred years ago it was believed that all the papyrus MSS had perished; none seemed to be in existence. Most of the papyrus MSS that have been found were discovered in the twentieth century.

Vellum MSS have also been discovered. The German scholar Constantin Tischendorf made an important discovery in 1844, when he was staying in a monastery on the slopes of Mount Sinai. He saw there some pieces of the Old Testament books from a very old Greek MS. It was not until his third visit to the monastery, fifteen years later, however, that Tischendorf saw the rest of the MS, including the New Testament and some Apocryphal books. The monks gave the MS to the Tsar of Russia, and eventually it was bought by the British Museum in London where it can be seen today. This MS, now called the *Codex Sinaiticus*, was probably made around AD350, and is one of the most valuable texts of the New Testament in existence.

Another vellum MS, perhaps even older than *Codex Sinaiticus*, is *Codex Vaticanus*, which has been in the Vatican for at least 500 years. Because there was hostility between the Roman Catholic Church and the Protestant Churches very few Protestant scholars were allowed to see it. In 1843 Tischendorf was allowed to look at it for just six hours. However in 1888–90 the whole of *Codex Vaticanus* was photographed and the photographs were published.

2 AIR TRAVEL AND MICROFILM

When Tischendorf travelled from Germany to Mount Sinai he had a long and difficult journey by sea and land. Today when a textual scholar wants to go and study a MS in Cairo, all he has to do is obtain permission and take a plane. If he wishes, he can even study the MS without travelling at all; it can be photographed on to microfilm and the microfilm can be sent to him by post. Modern inventions like aeroplanes and microfilm mean that a textual expert today is able to study nearly all the MSS that he wants to.

3 BETTER CO-OPERATION BETWEEN CHURCHES

There are still deep divisions between the Roman Catholic Church and the Protestant Churches, but there is much more co-operation between them than in the past. Today Roman Catholic and Protestant scholars work together on the text of the Bible, and share the results of their studies.

TEXTUAL VARIATIONS

THE ENDING OF MARK'S GOSPEL

We began this chapter by looking at the footnote at the end of Mark's Gospel. The very oldest MSS so far discovered end at Mark 16.8. The 'other ancient authorities' which do *not* have vv. 9–20 include *Codex Sinaiticus* and *Codex Vaticanus*, and it seems certain that those twelve verses were not in the autograph MS. However, Christians have been reading those verses for hundreds of years, so that many people consider they should be included in our Bibles, whether Mark actually wrote them or not. This is the reason for the various brackets, footnotes and italics at the end of Mark's Gospel.

THE WOMAN CAUGHT IN ADULTERY

There is similar uncertainty about the story of the woman caught in adultery (John 7.53—8.11). In most Bibles we find the story at the beginning of chapter 8 in John's Gospel, usually with a footnote, sometimes in brackets as well. Other Bibles give the whole story in a footnote. In the ancient MSS the story is found in different places. *Codex Sinaiticus* does not have it at all, nor does *Codex Vaticanus*. Some MSS have the story at the end of John's Gospel, and in a few it appears after Luke 21.38. This story about Jesus is an ancient one, but it seems certain that it was not an original part of John's Gospel. Jerome included it in the Vulgate, and most Christians would not like to have it removed from their Bibles.

These are two of the most notable variations in the text of the New Testament. They should not lead us to think that there is doubt about large sections of the New Testament. Most of the variations are very small, just a matter of spelling, or the order of the words.

STUDY SUGGESTIONS

WORDS AND MEANINGS

1. Explain the meaning of the following words:
   (a) footnote   (b) manuscript   (c) autograph manuscript
2. What is the meaning of the word 'conclude' in the sentence. 'One ancient authority concludes the book by adding after verse 8 the following passage.'?
3. What is the difference between a roll or 'scroll' and a 'codex'.
4. What is the revival of learning in Europe which began in the 15th century AD commonly called, and why?
5. What is the movement which resulted in the separation of the Protestant Churches from the Roman Catholic Church commonly called, and why?

REVIEW OF CONTENT

6. Explain why so few papyrus MSS of the New Testament have survived.
7. Give two reasons why the early Christians changed from using rolls to using codices.
8. (a) What was vellum made from?
   (b) What advantage did vellum have over papyrus?
9. What is meant by the term 'ancient authority' as used in the footnotes in many Bibles?
10. Why are there no autograph MSS of the New Testament books in existence?
11. Explain why the oldest MSS are not necessarily closest to the original.
12. Why was the invention of printing so important for the spread and study of the Gospel?
13. What is *Codex Sinaiticus*, where is it now, and how did it get its name?

BIBLE STUDY

14. Look up the footnotes in the RSV for the following verse, and say in each case what difference, if any, the alternative reading makes to the meaning of the verses.
    (a) Matt. 27.16   (b) Mark 1.1   (c) Mark 2.16   (d) Luke 3.22
    (e) John 5.2   (f) Acts 15.29   (g) Romans 8.28   (h) Rev. 13.7

FURTHER STUDY AND DISCUSSION

15. Into which languages is the New Testament being translated in your country? Are the translators able to translate from the Greek? If not, what other language do they translate from? What effect can this have on people's understanding of Scripture?
16. What would you say to a person who argued: 'Forget about all those footnotes and cross-references at the bottom of the page! It is the Bible text itself that matters.'
17. How important is a knowledge of New Testament Greek for a proper understanding of the New Testament? How far can we rely on translations for our own study of the Bible?

TRANSLATIONS

'All of us hear them speaking in our own languages of the great things that God has done.' (Acts 2.11)

So far we have been chiefly concerned with the Greek text of the New

Testament. However, there are very few Christians anywhere who can actually read the New Testament in Greek, and fortunately they do not need to. The good news about Jesus has been in translation ever since the day of Pentecost.

Christians have always felt free to translate the gospel message. The Gospel writers themselves translated the Aramaic words of Jesus into Greek, and we have seen that as soon as there was a need for it, the Greek was translated into Latin, and some of the ancient languages of eastern Europe, the Near East and North Africa (see p. 113). But the Latin Bible was so widely used that from the 9th to the 14th century only twenty or so translations of the Bible, or parts of it, were made in the languages of Western Europe. There have, however, been two main periods of Bible translation:

1. At the time of the Reformation new Protestant versions were called for in most of the major European languages;

2. In this present (20th) century the spread of literacy, following the world-wide expansion of the Church over the previous 150 years, created a need for Bibles in the indigenous languages of Asia, Africa, the Pacific, and to a lesser extent North and South America.

Today the New Testament or parts of it can be read in more than 1,800 languages. At the end of 1986, 935 translations of the complete New Testament were available, and the work of translating the whole Bible continues. For people who want it in English, there are many translations to choose from.

ENGLISH VERSIONS

According to the historian Bede, Anglo-Saxon paraphrases of Bible stories, for singing to the accompaniment of the harp, were composed by the poet Caedmon and Abbot Aldhelm of Malmesbury as early as the 7th and 8th centuries. Few people in Britain then could read, but during the next few centuries the Gospels, Psalms, the Ten Commandments and parts of the Pentateuch were translated into Anglo-Saxon for use in preaching.

The earliest translation of the complete Bible into English was made in the fourteenth century by John Wycliffe and his friends, who translated from the Latin before the invention of printing. The first printed New Testament in English appeared early in the 16th century, translated by William Tyndale from Erasmus's Greek text (see p. 114), but in order to get his translation published Tyndale had to leave England and go to Germany. Many Church leaders were afraid of what might happen if people were able to read the Bible in their own language, and they persecuted Bible translators. Tyndale was captured and executed as a heretic because of the work he had done. During the following seventy-five years, nine more translations of the New Testament into English were made, and seven translations of the Old Testament. The English rulers and bishops eventually accepted that the Bible in English had come to stay.

In 1604 the English bishops met King James I and asked him to authorize a new translation of the Bible which would have the approval of the English Church. The King agreed, and more than fifty scholars worked to make the new translation. They translated the New Testament from the Greek, and the Old Testament from the Hebrew. The result was the *Authorized Version* (AV), also called the 'King James Bible', which was published in 1611. For the next three centuries most English-speaking Protestants used the Authorized Version, though a number of other translations were made during that period. Roman Catholics used the Douai-Reims Bible, a translation of the Latin Vulgate completed in 1609.

MODERN TIMES

In the twentieth century there has been a renewed interest in Bible translation. The discovery of many of the ancient MSS has given scholars a better knowledge of the Bible text, and the English language has changed considerably over the last three centuries. For both these reasons new translations were needed. In the 1880s the Authorized Version was revised and the *Revised Version* was published (the New Testament in 1881 and the complete Bible in 1885), and since then at least twenty-six other English New Testament versions have appeared. Some were made by groups of scholars working together, others were by individuals.

Some of the translations are revisions, in which the translators tried to keep as close as possible to the words of an earlier translation (e.g. the *Revised Version* and *Revised Standard Version* – see p. 126). Others are completely new.

The translators of both the *New English Bible* (representative of the Anglican, Methodist, Baptist, and the then Presbyterian and Congregationalist Churches, and other Protestant Churches and the Bible Societies) and of the *Jerusalem Bible* (mostly Roman Catholics) produced entirely new translations based on recent research. Both these versions use present-day language rather than the traditional 'biblical' English of the revisions. The same is true of the more recent *New International Version* made by scholars from a number of more Conservative and Evangelical Churches, who also aimed at preserving some continuity with the long tradition of Scripture translation into English.

There are also some versions which are not really translations at all, but 'paraphrases', in which the 'translators' have not only put the text into English, but tried at the same time to clarify its meaning. An example of this is the *Living Bible*, which is one man's interpretation of what the original Bible writers meant to say, not a 'translation' in the usual sense of the word.

THE WORK OF TRANSLATORS

Translators of the New Testament do not have an easy job. First, they have to decide which of the Greek texts to translate from, and secondly, they have to decide the most accurate way of translating the text into another language.

WHICH TEXT TO TRANSLATE?

When there are differences between the ancient Greek texts, the translators must decide what principles to follow in selecting the one they are going to use. Here is an example of the problems they face.

'Once he was approached by a leper, who knelt before him begging his help. "If only you will," said the man, "you can cleanse me." In warm indignation Jesus stretched out his hand, touched him and said, "Indeed I will; be clean again" (Mark 1.40, NEB)

When the translators of the NEB translated Mark 1.40 they followed a different text from the usual one. The RSV translators followed earlier translations, and wrote 'was moved with pity' where the NEB has 'in warm indignation'. The Good News Bible – also sometimes called Today's English Version – has 'Jesus was filled with pity', but it adds a footnote – 'pity; *some manuscripts have anger.*'

In Mark 1.40 most of the ancient MSS have a word which means 'pity', but a few MSS have a different word, meaning 'anger'. The NEB translators decided to follow the texts which had 'anger'. Their reason was something like this: Possibly a scribe who was copying St Mark's Gospel saw 'anger' and thought it was a mistake; perhaps he changed it, and wrote 'pity' instead. Surely, the translators thought, no scribe would see 'pity' and change it to 'anger', he would want to make the text easier to understand, not harder. So the NEB translators decided that 'anger' was more likely to have been the word that Mark originally used.

The scholars who worked on the GNB translation decided to follow the majority of texts, which have 'pity', but they added the footnote because they knew there were good reasons for thinking that Mark *might* have written 'anger'.

WHICH PASSAGES TO INCLUDE?

Translators have to decide whether or not to include passages about which there is some doubt, such as Mark 16.9–20 and John 7.53—8.11. As we saw (pp. 111, 117), early editions of the RSV gave these passages as footnotes, but more recently they have been put back into the text, with footnotes saying 'other ancient authorities omit this passage'. Many of the Protestant Reformers disapproved of the Apocrypha (see ch. 6). They considered the Apocrypha inferior, as lacking the authority of the books of the Hebrew canon. So although there were Protestant translations of the Apocrypha, the translators began the practice of placing the Apocryphal books in a separate collection, between the Old and New Testaments. One English Bible widely used in the late 16th century was published without the Apocrypha, and in time it became rare for English Bibles to include the Apocrypha. The British and Foreign Bible Society, founded in 1804, even agreed not to publish Bibles containing the Apocryphal books. However, English versions with the Apocrypha and Deuterocanonical books in their original positions among the books of the Old Testament continued to be produced for Roman Catholic use, and today it is once again becoming common for English Bibles to contain the Apocrypha (see p. 87).

WHICH WORDS TO USE

Having decided which Greek text to use, translators must then decide how best to translate the Greek. There is no disagreement about the Greek text of John 1.5, yet in each English version it has been translated differently (see the comparative table on p. 123). The English translations do not even seem to mean the same thing!

A translator must try to understand the mind of the writer. When John wrote '*katalaben*' did he mean the darkness did not understand the light, or did he mean that the darkness did not put the light out? Or did he carefully choose that word just because it could have both meanings? The translator has to decide.

Translators may also be influenced by the way a word is used in the Church of their own time. For example, the Greek word 'baptizo' means to 'dip' or 'wash', but it has come to have a technical 'Church' meaning as well: to 'baptize'. So Bible translators have to decide which English word should translate it.

When we read the Bible in a translation we depend on the careful work which the translators have done in trying to pass on the meaning that the original writers intended.

CHOOSING A TRANSLATION

The great number of English translations now available can be very confusing, though not all of them are available in every country, and some are more popular than others. The choice will depend partly on the taste of individual Christians, and also on the taste and theological

TRANSLATIONS OF JOHN 1.5

Greek Text
καὶ τὸ Φψσ ἐυ τῇ δκοτία Φαίυει, καὶ ἡ δκοτία
αὐτὸ οὐ κατέ λα βεν.

Authorized Version (AV) 1611
And the light shineth in the darkness; and the darkness
comprehended it not.

Revised Version (RV) 1881
And the light shineth in the darkness; and the darkness
apprehended[3] it not.
[3]or overcame

Revised Standard Version (RSV) 1952 (and Ecumenical Edition
1973)
The light shines in the darkness, and the darkness has not
overcome it.

Jerusalem Bible (JB) 1966
A light that shines in the dark,
a light that darkness could not overpower.

New English Bible (NEB) 1970
The light shines on it in the dark, and the darkness has never
mastered it.

Good News Bible (GNB/TEV) 1976
The light shines in the darkness, and the darkness has never
put it out.

New International Version (NIV) 1978
The light shines in the dark, but the dark has not understood[a]
it.
[a]or overcome.

New Jerusalem Bible (NJB) 1985
and light shines in darkness
and darkness could not overpower it.

Living Bible (Paraphrase) 1971
His life is the light that shines through the darkness—and the
darkness can never extinguish it.

'When we read the Bible we depend on the careful work that translators have done' – and continue to do as language changes. In Swahili, for example, several different versions, in different forms of the language, followed the earlier translations made at the end of the 19th century, which were printed in the Arabic script used by traders before the spread of literacy in East Africa. The teacher explaining the parable of the Prodigal Son in a Tanzanian primary school has written out Luke 15.21 in a more modern version, from the Union Swahili Bible published in 1952.

standpoint of local and national Churches. One Church prefers one translation, another Church prefers a different one.

Most Christians have a version of the Bible which they like the best – usually the translation with which they feel most at home, and have heard from childhood. Or it may be the one which they find the easiest to read and understand. Here we shall take a closer look at three of the most widely used versions.

THE AUTHORIZED VERSION (AV) ALSO CALLED THE KING JAMES BIBLE (KJB)

This is the translation authorized by King James I for use in the Church of England (see p. 120), which is the reason for both of its names. It is the Bible which many English people know and love best, because until very recently it was the version normally read aloud in Church services. People learned to recite verses and even whole chapters of it by heart.

Some people think that because it is older than most of the other English translations ordinarily available in bookshops, and is written in old-fashioned English, the AV must be closest to the original Greek. But this is not true. As we have seen, two important changes have occurred during the several centuries since the AV was translated.

(a) For one thing, *the English language has changed.* We no longer use words like 'thou' and 'ye' when we talk to people, and over the years many words have completely changed their meanings. For example, in the 17th century to 'let' meant to 'hinder' or 'prevent', i.e. the opposite of its present-day meaning to 'allow' or 'permit'. And in the 17th century to 'prevent' meant to 'go in front' or to 'lead', i.e. quite different from its present-day meaning to 'stop' or 'hinder'. Thus the AV has 'Oftentimes I purposed to come unto you, but was *let*' [i.e. prevented] 'hitherto' (Rom. 1.13), and 'We which are alive and remain unto the coming of the Lord shall not *prevent*' [i.e. go in front of, or before] 'them which are asleep' (1 Thess. 4.15). Again, in 1611 'conversation' meant 'conduct' or 'behaviour'; it included what people *did*, not merely what they *said* (2 Cor. 1.13). So the words of the AV do not always mean what we expect them to mean, and it can be a difficult translation to understand. We can easily mistake its meaning without knowing it.

(b) As we saw (p. 116), *modern scholars have learnt a great deal more about the ancient Greek (and Hebrew) texts* of the Bible than it was possible for the 17th century translators to know. Not only have important ancient MSS been discovered; modern technology has made it much easier for scholars today to study and compare the ancient texts.

Many people love the Authorized Version because the words are so familiar that they sound like music. But if we want a Bible that is easy to understand and also as close as possible to the meaning of the original text, we need to use a more modern translation.

THE REVISED STANDARD VERSION

The Revised Version (RV) of the New Testament, published in 1881, was a revision of the AV by American and English scholars working together, taking into account the new knowledge of the Greek text, and bringing some of the English words up to date. The Americans, however, would have liked to include more changes, and fourteen years later they published the American Standard Edition of the Revised Version, often called simply 'the American Standard Version' (ASV). Fifty years later still, this Standard Version was revised, to give us the Revised Standard Version (RSV), of which the New Testament was published in 1946 and the complete Bible in 1952. By then additional manuscripts had been found, and scholars had realized that the New Testament was written in *Koine* Greek, not classical Greek (see Vol. 1, ch. 2, on the languages Jesus spoke).

The RSV was not intended to be a new translation. The revisers wanted to keep as far as possible the simple classic English of the King James version, so that the RSV is full of familiar words and rhythms. At the same time it is in simpler and more modern English than the older versions, and is a careful, scholarly work, based on the best Greek texts. For these reasons the RSV is a popular translation, used in many schools and colleges.

In 1966 a 'Catholic' edition of the RSV was published, and at about the same time an annotated RSV with Apocrypha, which was the first English Bible to receive both Protestant and Roman Catholic approval. The RSV Ecumenical Edition or 'Common Bible' which followed in 1973, with the Apocrypha/Deuterocanonical books grouped between Old and New Testaments, was sponsored by the National Council of Churches of Christ in the USA and endorsed for general use by Protestant, Roman Catholic and Greek Orthodox Churches alike. (This is the version on which the TEF Study Guides are now based.)

THE GOOD NEWS BIBLE (GNB) ALSO CALLED TODAY'S ENGLISH VERSION (TEV)

The GNB is an entirely new translation into simple straightforward English, prepared and published by the United Bible Societies for use throughout the world. It is very easy to read, even for people who have not had much education, or whose grasp of English is not very strong. The translators were aiming at popular everyday language, and they avoided the use of old-fashioned biblical English altogether. For example, this is how Luke 1.31 appears:

RSV	GNB/TEV
'You will conceive in your womb and bear a son, and you shall call his name Jesus.'	'You will become pregnant and give birth to a son, and you will name him Jesus.'

The GNB is especially useful for new Christians who are not familiar with the words of the AV. It is in the ordinary language of today, just as the AV was in the everyday language of the early 17th century and the original New Testament writings were in the everyday Greek of the first century. The GNB has become popular in many Churches and Bible-study groups.

CHOOSING A BIBLE

Christians have to decide for themselves which Bible version is best for them, though some Churches may recommend particular translations for their members to use, or authorize a specific version for reading in Church services. Ministers and teachers often find it useful to work with two or three translations. Comparing the differences between them can help to clarify the meaning. Some people like to use one translation for study (perhaps marking specially important passages, or writing in their notes and comments on difficult words), and keep another translation for devotional use. The choice is partly a matter of individual taste, but it is also important for us to understand *why* the translations differ from each other. Understanding the differences helps us to choose wisely.

STUDY SUGGESTIONS

WORDS AND MEANINGS

1. Explain what a 'paraphrase' is.

REVIEW OF CONTENT

2. In what two periods have most translations of the Bible been made?
3. Whose work resulted in the first English Bible?
4. Which translation of the Bible was used by English-speaking Protestants for over 300 years?
5. Which translation of the Bible was used by English-speaking Roman Catholics for the same period?
6. Give two examples of English Bibles which are
   (a) revisions   (b) new translations.

BIBLE STUDY

7. Use an Authorized Version, an RSV and one of the more modern

versions and compare their translations of the following passages. In each case state which translation you find the easiest to understand, and which translation you like the best, and why you like it.

(a) Matt. 11.20–21   (b) John 8.13–15   (c) 1 Cor. 13.4–7
(d) Gal. 6.12–15   (e) Heb. 10.1–3

FURTHER STUDY AND DISCUSSION

8. Which translation(s) of the Bible
(a) is most easily available in your country?
(b) is used the most in the church which you attend?
What advantages and what disadvantages have you found in using different translations?

9. (a) Why do you think the Church leaders of the sixteenth century were afraid of the Bible being translated into the language of the people?
(b) In your own country, what advantages and disadvantages do you think have resulted from the Bible being made available to people in a language which they can understand?

10. What particular features would you look for, in choosing Bible translations to be used for:
(a) study?
(b) private devotional use?
(c) reading aloud in Church services?
(d) missionary outreach and evangelism?

11. How would you answer someone who asked, 'How can I believe that any translation of the Bible is inspired, since every one is different'?

12. How would you respond to people who made the following statements?
(a) ' "King James" English was good enough for St Paul. It's good enough for me.'
(b) 'The AV is the oldest, so it must be the best.'
(c) 'I would never give anyone a copy of the Authorized Version. It is too old-fashioned.'

Appendixes

1. GLOSSARY OF TECHNICAL TERMS

ALLEGORY: A method of teaching or expressing ideas by telling a story or showing a picture in which various details stand for something else, e.g. the story of the wicked tenants (Mark 12.1–11).

APOCALYPSE (APOCALYPTIC): A book which claims to reveal heavenly secrets about the coming of God's kingdom, which is expected soon.

APOCRYPHA: The books which were in the Septuagint, but were not in the Hebrew Scriptures accepted by the rabbis in Palestine.

APOSTLE: Literally, 'someone who is sent' (from the Greek title for an ambassador or messenger). The name was given to the twelve disciples after the resurrection. Paul used it to mean someone who was personally commissioned by the risen Christ. See John 20.21; Acts 1.8; Eph. 3.1–5.

ARAMAIC: The language which Palestinian Jews spoke in the time of Jesus.

ATONEMENT: Jesus' work of bringing man and God together: 'at-one-ment'.

CANON: The list of books that were accepted as Scripture.

CHRIST: The anointed one: '*Christos*' in Greek, '*Messiah*' in Hebrew. '*Christos*' is one of Jesus' titles, and came to be used as a part of His name – 'Jesus Christ'.

CIRCUMCISION: The removal by surgery of the foreskin of the penis. All Jewish boys were circumcised on the eighth day as a sign of being Jewish. 'The circumcised' means Jews. 'The circumcision party' (see e.g. Gal. 2.12) refers to Christian Jews who thought that all Christians should be circumcised and keep the Jewish law.

CODEX (pl. CODICES): An ancient manuscript made from folded sheets like a modern exercise book.

CONCORDANCE: an alphabetical list of words used in the Bible, giving the Books, chapters and verses where they occur. Very useful for finding references.

DIDACHE: A Greek word meaning teaching. Also the name of an early Christian writing, *The Didache of the Twelve Apostles*.

DISCIPLE: A learner or a follower. Used especially of the followers of Jesus.

ESCHATOLOGY: The doctrine of the 'last things'.

EVANGELIST: Someone who carries good news, especially anyone who preaches the good news about Jesus. Also a person who writes a Gospel.

EXILE: The period of Jewish history, from c.587–538BC, when many Jews were forced to live in Babylon.

FORM CRITICISM: A method of studying the Gospels which takes account of the 'form' of the stories, teaching, and other types of material in the text.

GEMARA: The rabbinic discussions of the Mishnah, which were later written down. Together with the Mishnah they form the Talmud.

GOSPEL: Good News, especially the good news about Jesus. Also a written account of Jesus' life, death and resurrection.

HELLENIST: (from Hellas = Greece.) A person who adopted the Greek way of life. In the New Testament it means a Greek-speaking Jew.

HERESY (from the Greek hairesis, meaning a set of principles or school of thought): Now used to mean an opinion, doctrine, or particular interpretation of Scripture which conflicts with the generally accepted teaching of the Church. A HERETIC is a person who holds such an opinion or doctrine.

HERODIAN: A supporter of King Herod.

KERYGMA: Proclamation or preaching. Especially the announcement of what God has done in Jesus.

MANUSCRIPT: A document written by hand. Nowadays the 'manuscript' of a book may be typed, but the word is not used for anything already printed.

MESSIAH: A Hebrew word meaning 'the anointed one'. The Jews were expecting God to send a Messiah to save them from their enemies.

MINISTRY: Jesus' ministry was the period of His life when He wandered about with the disciples, teaching and healing. The ministry of the Church is the service of all Christians.

MISHNAH: The Jewish oral law, collected and written down by Rabbi Judah ha-Nasi (AD135–c.220).

PAPYRUS: Paper made from reeds. The sheets were usually joined together to make a roll or 'scroll'.

PARABLE: A story or a picture with a meaning; a comparison or a riddle.

PASSION: Jesus' 'passion' means His suffering and death. A 'Passion Narrative' is an account of His passion.

PENTATEUCH: The five books of Moses: Genesis, Exodus, Leviticus, Numbers and Deuteronomy.

PHARISEE: A member of a Jewish religious group which placed great emphasis on keeping the Jewish law.

PROOF TEXT: An Old Testament text which seems to point to Jesus.

PROSELYTE: A Gentile who became a Jew, was circumcised, and was bound by the Jewish law.

RABBI: The Hebrew name for a teacher. Many rabbis were also Pharisees.

REFORMATION: The period, mostly in the sixteenth century, when attempts to reform the Church in Europe resulted in the separation of the Protestant Churches from the Roman Catholic Church.

RENAISSANCE: The revival of learning which took place in Europe in the fifteenth and sixteenth centuries.

SADDUCEE: A member of a Jewish religious group closely associated with the worship in the Temple in Jerusalem.

SANHEDRIN: The supreme council of the Jews.

SCRIBE: A person who writes. In the New Testament it usually refers to a man who was an expert in the Jewish law, as in 'scribes and Pharisees'.

SEPTUAGINT: The Greek version of the Old Testament, used by Greek-speaking Jews and early Christians. There were more books in the Septuagint than in the Hebrew canon.

SHEMA: The Jewish confession of faith. It is made up of three passages from the Law, but especially Deuteronomy 6.4–5.

SYNOPTIC: Looking at something from the same point of view. Because of the similarities between them, Matthew, Mark and Luke are known as 'the Synoptic Gospels'.

TALMUD: The book which contains the Mishnah and the Gemara. The authoritative guide to Jewish spiritual life.

TARGUMS: Aramaic Translations of the Hebrew Scriptures.

TEXTS: Early manuscripts of the Bible.

TORAH: The Hebrew word for 'law', commonly used to mean the first five books of the Bible.

VULGATE: (from the Latin 'editio vulgata'). The Latin translation of the Bible, made by Jerome in the fourth century AD.

ZEALOT: A Jewish freedom fighter against the Roman overlords in the first century AD.

131

2. COMMON ABBREVIATIONS

AD   Anno Domini, Latin for 'in the year of the Lord', referring to the years after the birth of Jesus.

AV   Authorized Version (of the Bible), also called the King James Bible.

a,b,c,   as in 'Luke 2.21a'. Used to divide up a verse when giving references: 'a' refers to the first half of the verse, 'b' refers to the second half of the verse; 'c' is only used when referring to the last part of a long verse.

b.   born, normally followed by the date of birth.

BC   Before Christ, referring to years before the birth of Christ.

BCE   Before the Common Era (the same as BC, see CE).

c.   *circa*, Latin for 'around', 'about', as in 'Papias, *c*.60–*c*.130'. Used when only the approximate time of an event is known, not the exact year or date.

CE   Common Era. Used by Muslims and other non-Christians to mean the same as AD.

cf.   *confer*, Latin for 'compare'.

d.   died.

e.g.   *exempli gratia*, Latin for 'for example'.

etc.   *etcetera*, Latin for 'and so on'.

f., ff.   following (singular and plural). Used in references to mean 'and the following one or more of the items numbered'. In Bible references 'f' usually means 'and the following verse or verses up to the end of the sentence'; 'ff' means up to the end of the paragraph' (as in 'Rom. 9.10f; Acts 6.8ff'). In other books it normally refers to the following page(s), paragraph(s) or line(s), according to the item numbered.

GNB   Good News Bible (see TEV).

ibid   *ibidem*, Latin for 'in the same place'. This is a reference to a work that has just been referred to.

i.e.   *id est*, Latin for 'that is'.

KJB   King James Bible (see AV).

JB   Jerusalem Bible.

LXX   Septuagint.

MS   Manuscript (pl. MSS).

NB   *Nota bene*, Latin for 'note well', 'take good note of'.

NEB New English Bible.

NIV New International Version (of the Bible).

NJB New Jerusalem Bible.

NT New Testament

op. cit. *opera citato*, Latin for 'in the work cited'. Used when giving a reference to a book that has already been referred to.

OT Old Testament

pl. plural.

q.v. *quod vide*, Latin for 'which see'.

RSV Revised Standard Version of the Bible.

RV Revised Version.

s. singular.

TEV Today's English Version (of the Bible), also sometimes abbreviated as GNB, for the Good News Bible.

v., vv. Verse, verses.

Key to Study Suggestions

Chapter 1. Why the Gospels were written (Pages 7–8)
1. See p. 3, line 5 from foot of page.
2. See p. 1, last line and p. 4, line 14.
3. See p. 2, line 10 from foot of page.
4. See p. 4, lines 22–26.
5. See p. 6, last para.
6. See p. 3, para. numbered 1.
7. (a) See p. 2, para. 2.
    (b) See p. 2, paras numbered 3–5.
8. See p. 6, para. 3, and also read Matt. 1—2; Luke 1—2.
9. See p. 4, para. 3.
10. See p. 6, para. (b).
11. See Acts 1.21, 22.
13. (a) See p. 3, paras. numbered 1–4. (b) See Acts 1.3.
14. See p. 1, para. 1.
15. See Matt. 21.12–13 and the parallel passages as shown in cross references in your Bible.

Pages 16–17
1. See p. 11, lines 9–13.
2. See p. 14, line 11.
3. See p. 15, lines 4–5.
4. See p. 14, line 7 from foot of page.
5. See p. 8, last 2 paras.
6. See p. 11, para. 5.
7. (a) See p. 12, last para. (b) See p. 14, para. 2.
8. See p. 14, lines 20–26.
9. See p. 15, para. 1.
10. (a) See p. 15, lines 14 and 13 from foot of page.
    (b) See p. 15, lines 5 and 4 from foot of page.
12. See Matt. chs 1 and 2. Luke chs 1 and 2.

Special Note A. (Pages 20–21)
1. (a) See p. 19, lines 1–3.
    (b) See p. 19, line 15.
2. (a) See p. 19, line 9.
    (b) and (c) See p. 19, line 19.
    (d) See p. 19, line 13.
    (e) See p. 19, line 26.
    (f) See p. 19, line 4 from foot of page.
3. See p. 19, lines 4–5.
4. See p. 19, section 3(a), 3(b).

5. See p. 19, section 4.
6. See p. 19, section 3(c).
7. (a) See p. 19, lines 9–12.
   (b) See v. 2 (according to Mark's account Peter, James and John were the only ones present).
   (c) To show Jesus as the son of God.
8. (a) Check cross-references in your Bible.

Chapter 2. The Gospel According to Mark (Pages 26–27)
1. See p. 22, para. 2.
2. See p. 22, para. 4.
3. (a) See p. 25, lines 18 and 31.
   (b) See p. 23, line 31; p. 27, question 12.
4. See p. 22, para. 2.
5. (a) See p. 22, paras. 3 and 4.
   (b) See p. 22, last para.
6. See p. 23, lines 2 and 3.
7. See p. 25, whole of section headed Details in the Gospel Stories.
8. Naming the eyewitnesses of an event is a way of saying that it really happened. See p. 19, para 1 (a).
9. (a) If the girl needed to eat, it showed that she was really alive and not a ghost.
   (b) The sabbath ended at sunset. See Vol. 1, p. 12.
   (c) Moses and Elijah were two leaders of Israel, and they represented the law and the prophets (see p. 82).
   (d) Mark records that Jesus blessed the bread and broke it at the Last Supper to show the theological significance of His coming death and resurrection. The evangelist seems to have seen the same significance in the miraculous feeding of the 5,000 and the 4,000.
10. (a) and (b) See p. 22, paras. 3 and 4.

Pages 32 and 34
1. (a) See p. 27, last two paras. and p. 28, para. 1.
   (b) See p. 30, lines 17–22 and p. 31, lines 27–31.
2. See p. 27, line 4 from foot of page.
3. See p. 29, para. 3.
4. See p. 31, para. 4.
5. See p. 28, para. 3.
6. See p. 25, whole of section headed Details in Gospel Stories; p. 29, para. 4; p. 31, last full para.
7. (a) According to Mark Jesus could do 'no mighty work' (i.e. miracles).

(b) Mark's account is longer than Matthew's (see p. 29, para. 3), and gives more detail of what Jesus *did* do.
8. Impatient.
9. They were ordinary human beings, weak and confused and far from perfect.

Chapter 3. The Gospel according to Matthew (Pages 44–45)
1. (a) See p. 39, line 1.
   (b) See p. 37, last 3 lines and p. 38, lines 1–3.
   (c) See p. 43, line 8 from foot of page.
3. See p. 35, para. 2.
4. (a) See p. 35, line 1.
   (b) See p. 35, lines 20 and 21.
   (c) See p. 35, lines 21–23.
5. (a) and (b) See p. 37, last para.
6. See pp. 38 and 39.
7. See p. 36, lines 9–7 from foot of page.
8. See p. 43.
9. (a) See p. 42, para. 5.
   (b) See p. 41, whole of section headed A Tendency to Legislate.
10. (a) Matthew's account is shorter and omits a number of details.
    (b) In Matthew's account the disciples call Jesus 'Lord' and ask Him to save them. In Mark's account they just call Jesus 'Teacher', and do not seem to expect that He can save them.
11. According to Matthew 19. 28 the Twelve will judge the world, but according to 1 Cor. all Christians will judge the world..

Chapter 4. Luke–Acts: A Book in Two Parts (Pages 56–57)
1. (a) See p. 48, line 7 from foot of page, and the plan of Luke's Gospel.
   (b) See p. 47, last para.
2. See p. 47, line 23.
3. (a), (b), (c), (d) See p. 46, whole of section headed Authorship.
   (e) See p. 47, whole of section headed 'Most Excellent Theophilus'.
4. See p. 48, para. (a).
5. See p. 49, whole of section headed A Historical Approach.
7. (a) See v. 24. (b) See v. 26. (c) See v. 56.
8. (a) See v. 37, Jesus ate in a Pharisee's house.
   (b) See vv. 39–52.
9. See Volume 1, p. 17, whole of section headed Scribes.

Pages 62–64
1. See p. 60, whole of section headed A Selective Account.

2. See p. 57, line 8 from foot of page.
3. Passover.
4. See p. 62, lines 1–2 and Philemon 24.
5. See pp. 57 and 58, whole of section headed A Theological Book.
6. See p. 58, last two lines and p. 59, lines 1–18.
7. See p. 62, lines 12–15.
8. (a) See p. 59, last two paras, and p. 60, line 1.
   (b) See p. 60, lines 10–12.
9. See p. 59, line 12 from foot of page.
10. See p. 60, whole of section headed A Geographical Approach.
11. See p. 60f, whole of section headed First Hand Information.
12. (a) and (b). See p. 62, last para. of text.
13. (a) See v. 26.
14. (a) See vv. 7, 11, 12, 13, 14, 16, 17.
    (b) See vv. 7, 12, 13, 14, 16.
15. See Acts 13. 6–8, 45, 50; 14.2, 5,19.

Chapter 5. The Gospel according to John (Pages 73–74)

1. (a) See p. 67, last line.
   (b) See p. 69, lines 16–26.
   (c) See p. 73, lines 14–18.
2. See p. 73, last para. of text.
3. See p. 65, whole of section headed Four Gospels.
4. See p. 66, para. 3.
5. See p. 67, last 2 lines and p. 68, para. 1.
6. See p. 73, para. 2.
7. (a) See p. 68, last para.
   (b) See p. 69, para. 1.
8. See p. 69, whole of section headed Jesus' Teaching in John.
9. See p. 71, whole of section headed Jesus the Son.

Pages 79–80

1 and 2. See p. 75, section headed Editor's Notes, para. 1.
3. See p. 75, section on Editor's Notes, para. 2.
4. See p. 77, lines 17–18 from foot of page.
5. (a), (b), (c), (d) See pp. 76–77 whole of section headed The Beloved Disciple.
   (e), (f) See p. 77, whole of section headed Other Leaders Called John.
7. In Acts 4.13 John the son of Zebedee is described as 'uneducated', which leads people to question whether he could have written a Gospel. But in John 7.14 it is stated that Jesus had never studied. 'Uneducated' and 'never studied' could

simply mean that neither man had studied to become a rabbi.
See Vol. 1, p. 30.

Chapter 6. The Old Testament in the New Testament (Pages 91–92)
1. (a) See p. 84, last para.
   (b) See p. 85, para. 1.
   (c) See p. 85, paras, 2 and 3.
   (d) See p. 81, lines 16–13 from foot of page.
2. See p. 82, para. 1.
3. See p. 82, para. numbered 2(b).
4. See p. 89, para. 5.
5. See pp. 83–84, paras, numbered 1–4.
6. See p. 82, para. 2.
7. See p. 82, para. numbered 2(a).
8. See p. 85, para. 2.
9. Matthew was using LXX, which has 'a virgin'. The English OT is translated from Hebrew, which has 'a young woman'.

Chapter 7. The Canon (Pages 104–105)
1. (a) See p. 95, last para. and p. 96, para. 1.
   (b) See p. 100, paras. 4 and 5.
   (c) See Glossary, p. 129.
2. (a) See p. 99, lines 5–6.
3. See p. 101, para. 4 and lines 9 and 8 from foot of page.
4. See pp. 93–94, numbered sections 1–5.
5. (a) See p. 99, lines 3–4.
   (b) See p. 99, lines 27–30.
6. See p. 100, para. 4.
7. See p. 100, last 15 lines (paras. numbered 1–3).
8. See p. 95, para. 3.
9. (a) See p. 95, para. 4; p. 97, para. 6.
   (b) See p. 96, section headed The First List.
10. See pp. 97 and 99, section headed The Guidelines, numbered paras. 1 and 2.
11. See pp. 101–104, whole of section headed Surviving Lists.

Special Note B. The Inspiration of the New Testament (Page 110)
2. (a) See p. 106, para. 1.
   (b) See p. 106, para. 4.
3. See pp. 107–108.

Chapter 8. Texts and Translations (Pages 117–118)
1. (a) See p. 111, lines 10–12 and 22–23.
   (b) See p. 111, line 7 from foot of page.

(c) See p. 111, last 4 lines and p. 112, lines 1–4.
2. See p. 111, opening quotation.
3. See p. 112, section headed Papyrus Scrolls and Volume 1, p. 82, section headed Writing Materials.
4. See p. 114, para. 3.
5. See p. 114, para. 4.
6. See p. 112, para. 4.
7. See p. 112, para. 3.
8. See p. 113, lines 2–4.
9. See p. 117, lines 3–6.
10. See p. 112, lines 2–4.
11. See pp. 113–114, section headed Copies of Copies.
12. See p. 114, section headed Printed Bibles.
13. See p. 116, para. 3.

Pages 127–128
1. See p. 120, last para.
2. See p. 119, paras. numbered 1 and 2.
3. See p. 119, last para.
4 & 5. See p. 120, para. 2.
6. See p. 120, section headed Modern Times.
9. (a) See p. 119, lines 5–3 from foot of page.
12. See pp. 123 and 125, section headed The Authorized Version.

Index

This index includes most of the subjects dealt with in this Guide, and the names of important people and places mentioned. Page numbers with an asterisk refer to the Glossary, where certain words are defined more fully than in the text.

140